PRAISE FOR

Birds of Crater Lake National Park:
A Natural History and Guide

"*Birds of Crater Lake National Park* is a welcome and overdue description of the birds of this majestic national park. Information on the region's geology, climate, and floristic diversity meld wonderfully to give the background needed to appreciate the descriptions of the park's avian biota and the latter's dependence on the varied habitats found in the park. Stewart Janes is a knowledgeable naturalist who conveys the beauty of the connection of birds to their surroundings. This guide will enhance the experience of all who want to delve deeper and experience the park to its fullest through its birds."

> —DR. MICHAEL T. MURPHY, professor emeritus of biology, Portland State University

"The visitors who flock to Crater Lake for its scenic beauty have long needed a guide to the diverse and fascinating birds that call the park their home. *Birds of Crater Lake National Park* provides a comprehensive introduction to the park's birds and describes the adaptations that allow them to thrive. With illuminating descriptions of the park's varied habitats, this book will be an invaluable companion for every visitor interested in learning more about the natural history of Crater Lake."

> —DR. PEPPER TRAIL, retired forensic scientist and ornithologist at the US Fish and Wildlife Service Forensics Laboratory in Oregon

BIRDS OF CRATER LAKE NATIONAL PARK

Phantom Ship, Crater Lake

Birds of Crater Lake National Park

A NATURAL HISTORY AND GUIDE

Stewart Janes

Photographs by Jim Livaudais

Oregon State University Press   Corvallis

Generous support from the John and Shirley Byrne Fund for Books on Nature and the Environment helped make publication of this book possible.

Cataloging-in-publication information is available from the Library of Congress.
ISBN 978-1-962645-49-2 paper; ISBN 978-1-962645-50-8 ebook

∞ This paper meets the requirements of ANSI/NISO Z39.48-1992 (Permanence of Paper).

First published in 2026 by Oregon State University Press
Printed in the United States of America

Oregon State University
OSU Press

Oregon State University Press
121 The Valley Library
Corvallis OR 97331-4501
541-737-3166 • fax 541-737-3170
www.osupress.oregonstate.edu

Oregon State University Press in Corvallis, Oregon, is located within the traditional home-lands of the Marys River or Ampinefu Band of Kalapuya. Following the Willamette Valley Treaty of 1855, Kalapuya people were forcibly removed to reservations in Western Oregon. Today, living descendants of these people are a part of the Confederated Tribes of Grand Ronde Community of Oregon (grandronde.org) and the Confederated Tribes of the Siletz Indians (ctsi.nsn.us).

Contents

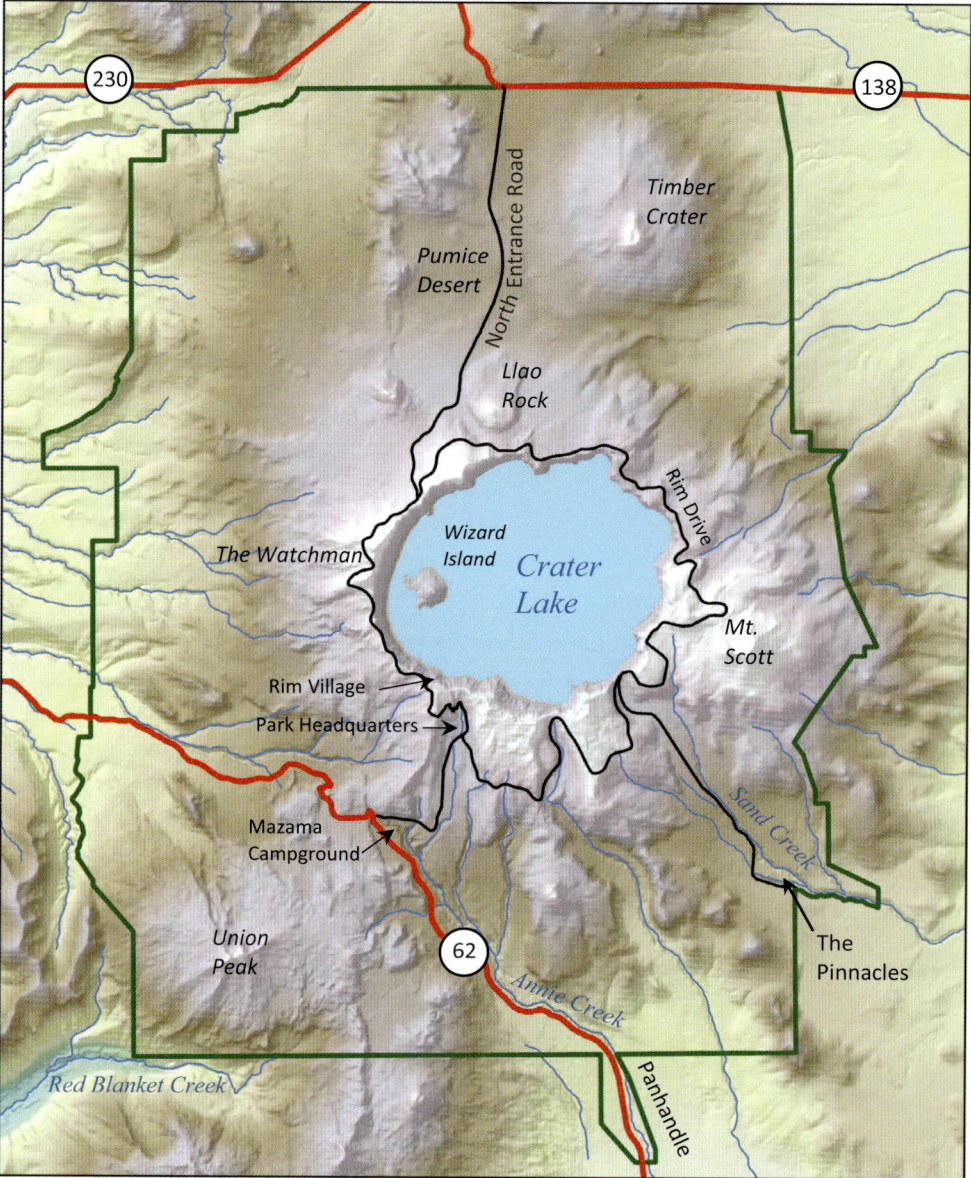

230

138

Timber
Crater

Pumice
Desert

North Entrance Road

Llao
Rock

Rim Drive

The Watchman

Wizard
Island

*Crater
Lake*

Mt.
Scott

Rim Village

Park Headquarters

Sand Creek

Mazama
Campground

The
Pinnacles

Union
Peak

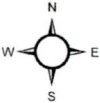

62

Annie Creek

Panhandle

Red Blanket Creek

Elevation (feet)

8930

3260

N

W   E

S

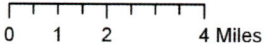

0   1   2   4 Miles

Acknowledgments

Many people assisted in making this volume possible. I am grateful to Frank Lang, a mentor who watched as I worried over the manuscript and warned me not to wait too long. I am also grateful to those who shared their expertise, enriching my knowledge of various aspects of the area's natural history, including Lee Ryker (entomology), Jad D'Allura (geology), Mark Buktenica (aquatic ecology), and Jeff LaLande (history). Thanks to Marshall Gannett for his skill in producing the map. And, of course, I am indebted to Debbie, my wife, who offered encouragement and read numerous editions, editing and proofing each.

Introduction

Birds that inhabit Crater Lake and the surrounding high country face great challenges. This might not be apparent on a sunny summer day, with the view of Wizard Island rising from the blue water and the last snowfields melting from the slopes. The high country is an energy-poor and hostile environment.

Humans face day-to-day challenges of all kinds. Sitting at home with a cup of coffee in hand contemplating the chores and events of the coming day likely includes at least some small measure of stress. The odd noise in the car will likely mean arranging an inconvenient trip to the mechanic. Will there be time to stop by the pharmacy before the kids get home? Will there be enough money for the hoped-for vacation?

Valid concerns, but all pale in comparison with the stress facing birds in the field and forest at all elevations. Foremost is the challenge of securing sufficient food to survive the night. Birds have a very high metabolism, and overnight survival is not certain, especially for the smallest.

Birds also have a host of predators to avoid. For a small bird like a warbler, a mortality rate of 1 percent a month in a resident population is typical. This might not seem that great until you consider there are twelve months in the year. It quickly adds up.

The timberline in the Pacific Northwest lies at about 6000 feet elevation, varying somewhat with aspect and latitude. It marks the elevation above which dense forests are unable to survive, leaving a hardy few like whitebark pines (*Pinus albicaulis*) and mountain hemlocks (*Tsuga mertensiana*) to endure the punishing winter winds and abrasive blowing ice. Much of Crater Lake National Park lies above timberline, including most locations frequented by visitors. The elevation of the lake's surface is 6200', and the surrounding rim ranges from 6700' to 7800'. Although the Cascades are not as high as many of the mountainous areas in the west, the climate of the Pacific Northwest ensures generous precipitation and a cloak of snow that persists well into the summer. At high elevations, life is challenging for nearly all inhabitants. Plants, invertebrates, mammals, and birds must contend with conditions that a great many cannot survive.

I spent much of my career as an ornithologist exploring and researching the birds that inhabit the mountains and valleys of southern Oregon. Ascending the slopes of Mount Mazama, the mountain that contains Crater Lake, and other mountains in the region, species after species reach an elevational limit, continuing no farther into the high country. The birds living at higher elevations stand out for their ability to survive in harsh conditions. I remember clearly the tiny Golden-crowned Kinglet I encountered while it foraged at the rim of Crater Lake among the branches of a mountain hemlock in January with a cold, stiff wind blowing. It just didn't seem possible that a bird weighing less than a quarter of an ounce could survive. I considered this as I was forced to retreat with my well-insulated clothing to a warm car and a thermos of hot cocoa.

Birds that inhabit Crater Lake National Park and the high country of the mountain west are a remarkable set of species. This includes the birds that abandon the high country for more benign environments for the winter. More than their lowland cousins, they must contend with bitter storms, a brief and often unpredictable growing season, poor soils that produce limited resources, and nights that can drop below freezing at any time of year.

Each species that lives here has adaptations and strategies that allow it to succeed in this environment. Some have incredible memories, some of the best in the entire animal world. They can remember where they cached food a year earlier. An excellent memory is quite helpful when snow covers much of the high country for seven months of the year or more, and most potential food is concealed. Several species of birds employ a wide diversity of foraging techniques that demonstrate greater flexibility than those of their relatives in more accommodating and productive environments. This flexibility is vital when resources are thinly spread and ephemeral for much of the year. Others exhibit diverse strategies for conserving precious energy (food) harvested from an energy-poor environment. For example, a few allow their body temperature to drop when roosting, permitting them to survive a long and cold night and greet another dawn.

For a brief time each year, the high country is more welcoming. It fills an important need for birds breeding in the gentler climate at lower elevations throughout the broader region. As the usual summer drought sets in, many food resources become scarce. This is time for the annual molt and preparation for the journey to wintering areas far to the south. The tardy burst of productivity that occurs at higher elevations invites a range of both insectivorous birds and raptors to find the resources they need.

Crater Lake is a unique treasure not only for Oregon but also for the world. The lake, with its remarkable clarity, resides within a caldera unlike any other and invites many thousands of visitors to enjoy the sight each year. A select few visit the park in winter to brave the cold for an exhilarating snowshoe or cross-country ski outing. However, most choose to visit after the Rim Drive opens to automobile traffic, in late June in most years. There is still snow about, but in the warming sun at the Watchman, or Cloudcap, or any of the other viewpoints around the rim, it is easy to forget the harsh conditions that envelop the park much of the year.

This book will introduce you to the birds you are most likely to encounter on visits to Crater Lake National Park and elsewhere at high elevations throughout the west. I also offer accounts of a few species you are less likely to see but that reveal important stories about life in the high country. The book may serve as a field guide, helping to identify the birds you encounter, but more than that, I hope to provide insight into the life of the birds that call the high country home. Climate, elevation, and geology all interact to dictate the conditions on the mountain. Through their stories of survival, I hope to help readers appreciate and understand how the birds meet the twin challenges of limited food and adverse weather both seasonally and daily. I also hope this volume will serve as an enjoyable reminder of your experiences in the park and elsewhere in the high country and as an invitation to explore the birds and the natural history of the surrounding area.

A BRIEF HISTORY OF ORNITHOLOGY
AT CRATER LAKE NATIONAL PARK

In contrast to other areas in the west, awareness and understanding of the birds and wildlife inhabiting higher elevations encompasses a relatively brief span of time. The high country of the Cascade Mountains remained largely unexplored as the trappers and homesteaders of the 1700s and 1800s sought furs and arable land, respectively. The valleys provided the best opportunities, while the mountains were viewed largely as obstacles to be negotiated with the least possible effort. Travelers rarely strayed from the established routes through the passes.

Not until prospectors seeking their fortune stumbled across Crater Lake in 1853, led by John Hillman, did Europeans discover its existence. Unfortunately for them, extrusive volcanic rocks that make up the High Cascades yielded few precious metals. Fortunes, if they were made in the region, occurred to the southwest in the Klamath Mountains. The discovery of Crater Lake received little attention, in part due to confusion regarding the location of the lake, potential threats from Indigenous people in the area, and no regional newspaper to report the find.

Crater Lake was, of course, familiar to the Indigenous people. The Klamath people hunted and camped on Mazama's slopes. Crater Lake was known as Gewas to the Klamath people and was considered a place of spiritual power. Legends are shared about the battle between the gods Skell and Llao. The lake was considered a dangerous place for people not prepared to visit. Shamans were some of the few to visit the rim on "power quests."

The discovery of Crater Lake by Europeans made little impression on the homesteaders, if noted at all. The lake was "rediscovered" nine years later in 1862 by another group of prospectors headed by Chauncy Nye. Oregon had been admitted to the United States in 1859 without its residents realizing that it included this remarkable treasure.

The first ornithologist to visit the slopes of Mount Mazama and view Crater Lake was Major Charles E. Bendire. As part of the military after the Civil War, Bendire was stationed at a number of outposts throughout the west and made extensive collections of birds and eggs in each area he visited. In 1882 and 1883 he was stationed at Fort Klamath, just to the south of present-day Crater Lake National Park, and broadly surveyed the region. J. C. Merrill followed in 1886 and 1887 (Merrill 1888). Although their collections, now in the US National Museum, provide a valuable contribution to the knowledge of birds in the area, their records were often not detailed enough to place specimens at a specific locality or even to identify whether a given specimen was collected within the eventual boundaries of Crater Lake National Park.

The first serious effort to document the birds and mammals of the region was accomplished by the US Biological Survey in 1896, which sent an august team of biologists including C. Hart Merriam, Edward A. Preble, Vernon Bailey, and Cleveland Allen. Their work provided the first thorough look at the birds and mammals of what would later become Crater Lake National Park. Even so, not until the mid-1920s did biologists working at the new national park begin keeping consistent records of observations. The most complete record of birdlife at Crater Lake National Park was by Donald Farner, published in 1952.

Most recently, the National Park Service has embarked on an inventorying and monitoring program to document the biological diversity present on each of the units under their management, including Crater Lake National Park. The censuses conducted in the spring provide valuable information on breeding bird populations and provide baseline data by which to measure future changes in distribution and abundance.

CHANGES IN BIRD POPULATIONS SINCE 1952

In the years since Don Farner published *The Birds of Crater Lake National Park* in 1952, there have been changes in the bird communities that inhabit the park. Additional species have been recorded, and the list is sure to grow. Some are simply the result of more eyes and more time encountering the rare and hard to detect. Others reflect changes in climate and habitat that offer new opportunities for some or loss for others. There have been declines. For some the explanation is apparent, but for others it can be difficult to attribute reasons with any certainty. Some may involve a response to events occurring within the park, including biological succession or some disturbance, often fire. Other explanations may involve events with origins far beyond the park boundaries, including alterations to distant winter habitat. The following include some examples of changes noted since the time of Farner more than seventy years ago.

Prior to 1940, Red-shouldered Hawks were virtually unknown in Oregon. Gradually, they colonized the state arriving from California, beginning along the coast and later through the inland valleys. Today they occur broadly west of the Cascades and locally in riparian areas to the east. Individuals residing west of the Cascades remain on the breeding territory year-round. East of the Cascades, most migrate south for the winter. Small numbers pass over the park each August and September.

The Barred Owl is another recent addition to the park. The first Barred Owls were reported in Oregon in the early 1970s, having expanded their range across North America from their traditional home in the east. A survey reported in 2014 found six pairs within the park, apparently displacing Spotted Owls in the process (Mohren and Beck 2015). The expansion of the ranges of both the hawk and the owl may be a response to habitat alterations brought about by human activities or changes in climate.

In the early part of the 1900s, Anna's Hummingbirds were unknown in Oregon. The first Anna's Hummingbird was reported in 1944 in North Bend on the coast. By the late 1960s, they were widespread but uncommon residents west of the Cascades. Today they are common and even occur east of the Cascades in locations including Bend and The Dalles as summer residents. They now occur on occasion in the park.

The reason for the range expansion of the Anna's Hummingbird, which now extends into British Columbia, is due, in part, to the appearance of the "perpetual flower" in backyards of town and country: the hummingbird feeders installed by many that provide an endless supply of sugar water. Whereas in the past, when fall and winter meant a dearth of flowers, now a ready and predictable supply of food is available for this species, and they have been quick to take advantage. It is now a breeding species east of the crest of the Oregon Cascades, often far from the influence of feeders.

The most obvious addition to the list of breeding species is the White-crowned Sparrow. White-crowned Sparrows are widespread winter residents throughout the state at lower elevations, and many pass through the park in transit both north and south. In the breeding season they are more localized. White-crowned Sparrows are common along the coast among the beach grasses, where the grasses mix with shrubs. They also occur in openings in the foothills of the Coast and Cascade Ranges, frequenting recovering clearcuts and tree farms. They also breed at high elevations where forests give way to mountain meadows.

Farner found White-crowned Sparrows to be common migrants in the park but not as a breeding species. By the 1970s, Follett identified them as breeding in small numbers within the park. Today they are regular if uncommon breeders in the mountain meadows with willows around Munson Meadows.

It is doubtful that Farner would have missed this bird with its clear and distinctive song. Apparently, it is a new addition to the park. The habitat appears unchanged, so its earlier absence is difficult to explain. One possibility is that warmer temperatures on average mean earlier snowmelt. Just a few days can make the difference whether a bird (or plant or insect) can thrive in an area. This small change may have been enough to allow the White-crowned Sparrow to successfully complete its breeding cycle and colonize the park.

Others that have apparently increased their presence include Vaux's Swifts. Farner considered them to be rare and irregular visitors to the park. Today a stop along the rim in late August or September is likely to produce one or more small flocks speeding along as they head to wintering areas in Mexico.

Then there are the vagrants, those birds that for whatever reason turn up in the most unlikely places. For example, a Brown Pelican made a brief appearance on Crater Lake in 2006, perched on a buoy in the lake. Brown Pelicans rarely occur inland, seldom leaving salt water.

While there have been additions, there have been declines, too. Some birds common in the mid-twentieth century in the park have diminished in number.

The Double-crested Cormorant is a common bird on inland lakes of the region, from the Great Basin including Malheur National Wildlife Refuge and the lakes in Warner Valley and the Klamath Basin to those in the high country, such as Hyatt Lake to the south. Double-crested Cormorants are about three years of age before nesting for the first time. Even if they don't nest at a lake, immature birds will seek out the best fishing opportunities wherever they may be found.

Before fish were introduced to Crater Lake, there would have been little food for Double-crested Cormorants, and though they may have visited, it is unlikely they stayed long. The same would have been true for Bald Eagles and Common Mergansers. With the introduction of rainbow trout and kokanee in the late 1800s, as well as the introduction of crayfish (*Pacifastacus leniusculus*) to provide food for the fish, these birds were quick to exploit the new opportunities.

Seventy years ago, Double-crested Cormorants were regular visitors to the lake and even nested. Their numbers have apparently declined since, with fewer sightings. Apparently, fish populations are lower than in previous decades.

The Rufous Hummingbird is the common hummingbird in the park both during summer and into early fall as the post-breeding birds gather to feast on the abundant nectar supplies at the higher elevations in preparation for their migration to Mexico. Farner (1952) described them as abundant, and Follett (1979) considered them common. While they can still be considered common, their abundance has declined across their range (Wells 2007).

The same applies to the Olive-sided Flycatcher. Formerly considered common or relatively common in the park, it appears to have declined in recent decades across its range.

Farner recorded the Western Warbling Vireo as a regular breeding bird along Annie Creek. Where their songs were relentlessly repeated throughout the summer in the canyons, this voice has been largely missing from the chorus in recent years. It is unclear whether this is just normal variation in numbers experienced by many species or whether conditions have changed. If the decline is real, I suspect that an increase in Brown-headed Cowbird numbers may be at least in part responsible. The Brown-headed Cowbird was not recorded by Farner in the early 1950s. Indeed, the Brown-headed Cowbird was considered "not common" in the drier regions east of the Oregon Cascades in the early twentieth century and only a rare straggler west of the Cascades (Gabrielson and Jewett 1970). By the 1960s, the Cowbird was a widespread and common resident throughout except for more heavily forested regions. The reason for their expansion into the Pacific Northwest is unknown, but they are now a fixture, and the many species of birds with open cup nests are vulnerable to this brood parasite. Brood parasites are species that deposit their eggs in other bird's nests for the host to rear. The young of the host suffer as a result.

In the early part of the twentieth century, Williamson's Sapsuckers were apparently more common than Red-breasted Sapsuckers in the park. Williamson's Sapsuckers are found in a variety of conifers but with a preference for ponderosa pines (*Pinus ponderosa*, Marshall et al. 2003), and, as such, they are more common on the east side of the park. Red-breasted Sapsuckers were considered "somewhat uncommon" also at a variety of elevations and habitat but more common in the true firs (*Abies* spp.) and Douglas-firs (*Pseudotsuga menziesii*) to the west. Both may be found together at higher elevations. Today the pattern is reversed. The Red-breasted Sapsucker is the more common species, and the Williamson's Sapsucker is less common, to the point of being rather rare.

Fire is an important ecological force in the forests of southern Oregon. Beginning in the early twentieth century, forest managers began a campaign of preventing and quickly extinguishing fires in the forests. This effort to suppress fire has led to many changes, including the composition of the forests.

Along the eastern slopes of the Cascades, ponderosa pine is one of the most common trees. It is better adapted to lower precipitation. It is also adapted to fire. The bark is thick, and the tree self-prunes, leaving few limbs low to the ground. This makes it less likely that fire will rise into the canopy, killing the tree. With fewer fires, white fir (*Abies concolor*) and other species gradually invade much of the ponderosa pine habitat. This tends to make the habitat more suitable for Red-breasted Sapsuckers and less suitable to Williamson's Sapsuckers. This change may account for the change in the abundance of the two species. Fires are still actively suppressed in the park, especially where they threaten cultural resources.

The Green-tailed Towhee and Fox Sparrow were apparently more abundant in the past. Both were regularly reported singing and breeding in the shrubland near the Pinnacles and elsewhere in the southeastern quarter of the park. Today neither species is easily found unless one makes the effort to visit the eastern margins of the park.

Following a fire, shrubby species of plants recover quickly, especially if trees killed by the fire allow more light to reach the ground. The reduction in the incidence of fire over the last century has likely allowed the forest to encroach on the shrubland once more common within the borders of the park. As bitterbrush (*Purshia tridentata*), green-leaf manzanita (*Arctostaphylos patula*), and snowbrush (*Ceanothus velutinus*, often simply called ceanothus) decrease in density, the Green-tailed Towhee and Fox Sparrow numbers have apparently decreased. Both depend on the dense cover for shelter, nesting, and foraging. Both are specialized for scratching through the leaf litter that accumulates beneath the shrubs for both seeds and invertebrates.

Lazuli Buntings can be found breeding in the park every year, but like the tides, their range moves up and down the mountainside. Farner (1952) considered them to be "sporadically . . . fairly common," while Follett (1979) considered them to be rare in the park. In some years Lazuli Buntings can be found breeding right up to the rim above Crater Lake, while in other years one must travel some distance down the mountainside to find them. In recent decades, at least, they have been common in riparian habitat from the rim to the lowest elevations in the park. These changes are attributable, in part, to annual variations in snowpack and the arrival of spring.

Although changes are constantly taking place, they are seldom dramatic. The avifauna of the twenty-first century looks quite similar to the avifauna present when Don Farner worked at the park.

Future Changes

Further changes in the bird communities are inevitable. A warming planet with unpredictable consequences in weather patterns and changes in the fire regime involving frequency and intensity are just two factors likely to result in both gains and losses.

The future of the iconic Clark's Nutcracker at Crater Lake National Park is uncertain. A disease is exerting its influence, which may render the park an uninhabitable place for the Nutcracker. White pine blister rust (*Cronartium ribicola*) is a fungus of five-needle pines including western white pine (*Pinus monticola*), sugar pine (*P. lambertiana*), and whitebark pine. For more than fifty years, foresters have struggled to contain and eliminate this recent addition to Oregon's forests. The origins of the fungus are in the eastern white pine forests of eastern North America and, before that, Europe and Asia. Control efforts have included attempts at the eradication of its intermediate hosts, currants and gooseberries (*Ribes* spp.), but this has proven ineffective. For reasons that are unclear, it has only recently invaded the high country, threatening whitebark pine. Whitebark pines are now dying in the park because of the disease. No one knows just how profound the impact will be. Will the disease merely diminish the population of pines somewhat, or will the disease eliminate the species as an ecological presence, in effect eliminating a primary food source of the Clark's Nutcracker? To be sure, Nutcrackers consume other foods, including the seeds of other pines such as ponderosa and sugar pines. However, most alternative foods are restricted to lower elevations. It is conceivable that Clark's Nutcrackers may one day abandon the park.

The age of discovery is not over. The Boreal Owl is a secretive small owl related to the more familiar Saw-whet Owl. This cousin is usually associated with the boreal forests of Alaska and Canada. Yet isolated populations were recognized in the Rocky Mountains of Colorado. As the search has intensified, additional populations have been discovered in the high country throughout the west, including the Cascades of Oregon. Recently one was detected just to the west of the park boundary. It is quite likely that they also occur within the park. All it will take is someone with great patience and a love of snowshoes or cross-country skis to explore the park in early spring when these birds are calling.

THE SETTING

To understand the birds of Crater Lake National Park, you must first understand the mountain in which Crater Lake resides, Mount Mazama. To understand the mountain, you must consider the mountain in the larger context of its place and time on the planet.

Europeans have been in the Pacific Northwest for the briefest of instances, geologically speaking. We have seen little. It is hard for us to realize that we live during calamitous times, times of great upheaval and a restless earth. In my life and the lives of those I have known, Mount St. Helens has erupted and so has Mount Lassen. Other volcanoes have roused briefly to shake and shiver and vent steam, giving an indication of the unsettled and restless scene under our feet. Mount Baker, Mount Hood, and the Three Sisters have all put us on notice in recent decades, if we have bothered to pay attention. Earthquakes, though modest in size, are regular events and give further clue to the relentless changes that are going on around us.

Native American culture in the region has existed much longer, though still barely measurable on the geological time scale. In the 13,000 years or more that Indigenous peoples have lived in the Oregon country, they have seen much more and could testify more vividly to the restless landscape, including the eruption that gave rise to Crater Lake.

CLIMATE AND ITS ROLE

Crater Lake is located 43° north of the equator and close to the western coast of the continent. This is more than an address. It tells an ecologist a great many things about Crater Lake without ever having visited North America or seen a picture of Crater Lake or spoken to anyone of this place.

A rotating planet creates a complex pattern of horizontal and vertical motion of air within the atmosphere. To begin to understand these movements, it's easiest to begin at the equator. The sun shines most directly on the earth at the equator, on average. This heats the air at the surface, more so than at higher latitudes, and the heated air rises. Eventually the air cools and can rise no farther. It must go somewhere, because more heated air continually arrives from below. The air is forced to spread north and south. As it cools further, it becomes denser, and it begins to fall back to the surface of the earth. This occurs at about 30° north and south latitudes. Some of the air splashing on to the surface of the earth north of the equator returns to the south, replenishing the air rising at the equator (events south of the equator mirror those in the north). The air heading south from 30° north creates the dependable northeast trade winds. The rest of the air mass spilling on to the earth's surface at 30° north latitude heads north toward the park.

Other less well-defined wind patterns occur at higher latitudes, to the north of Crater Lake, but much of the air at the surface comes south toward Crater Lake. Between 40° and 60° latitude, air masses moving north and south converge, and the spinning of the earth bends these winds around so that they consistently arrive from the west. This bending of the winds due to the rotation of the earth is called the Coriolis effect.

Thus, when we want to predict tomorrow's weather, we first look to the west. The winds blowing long over the Pacific Ocean gather abundant moisture evaporating from the surface. The often-saturated air blows on to the continent and, in Oregon, first encounters the Coast Range. These mountains are far from impressive, especially when compared to the high Cascades just to the east. Still, they are big enough to have a huge impact on climate.

Pressure and temperature are closely related. Increasing pressure increases temperature, just as decreasing pressure leads to reduced temperature. We see this in many ways in our daily lives, though most of us are unaware. If we pump up a tire, the tire becomes warm to the touch. When we pop the top of a soda can, releasing the pressure, the temperature in the gas in the can above the soda plunges below freezing, if only for a moment. This is the principle behind refrigerators, heat pumps, and air conditioners. Compressors pressurize the coolant, raising its temperature. Releasing the pressure permits the coolant to cool. Depending on where you let each of these events take place, you can heat or cool a space as desired.

Now we are almost ready to consider the effect of the westerlies meeting the Coast Ranges, but we need one more piece of information. The higher up you go in elevation, the lower the air pressure. You notice this when your ears "pop" going over a mountain pass. As you go up, more of the earth's atmosphere is below you. Thus, there is less weight of the air above you pressing down. We do not notice the tons of pressure pressing in on our bodies because it is always there.

Now visualize an air mass coming from the west and encountering the Coast Ranges. The air must rise a couple of thousand feet to scale the mountains to continue the journey east. By rising that modest amount, the pressure drops and so does the temperature. Cooler air cannot hold as much moisture. So, clouds form, if they haven't already, and it rains. Many visitors to the Oregon coast wonder if the sun ever shines. Many longtime residents wonder, too. The abundant rain gives rise to the temperate rainforest, with towering trees and a rich tangle of vegetation. All of this happens because of latitude, location at the western edge of the continent, and a modest set of mountains. This rainfall pattern goes by the name of orographic precipitation, literally "mountain rains and snow."

The air mass approaches Crater Lake within the Cascades, still from the west. The air mass now rises again, this time higher, to negotiate the Cascades. The rising air cools further. More precipitation is squeezed from the air, not only as rain but often as snow.

The air mass, having been wrung of its moisture, continues to the east as a relatively dry air mass. Therefore, the land east of the Cascades receives little rain and snow. Little moisture is left in the air, creating sagebrush country and the high desert. On a finer scale, this is why the western portion of Crater Lake National Park is wetter and lusher than the portion east of the crest of the Cascades. The air scaling the slopes in the west releases much of its moisture, while the air sliding off the eastern slopes does not. This difference in precipitation leads to profound differences in vegetation and in the birds that occur here.

Hermit Warblers, Chestnut-backed Chickadees, Red-breasted Sapsuckers, and Western Flycatchers tend to be found on the moister slopes of the park to the west. In contrast, Common Nighthawks, White-headed Woodpeckers, Dusky Flycatchers, Green-tailed Towhees, and Fox Sparrows tend to be found only on the drier eastern slopes of the park.

The pattern described above would suffice if the earth's axis of rotation was perpendicular to its plane of orbit around the sun. Then the equator would always receive the most direct sunlight, and there would be no seasons. It would always be the first day of spring (or fall). However, the earth's axis is tilted 23.5° with respect to its plane of orbit. This means that the sun is directly overhead at different latitudes on different dates. On the first day of summer, the summer solstice, it is directly over the Tropic of Cancer (23.5° N latitude). Days are long and nights are short at Crater Lake. Six months later, the sun is directly over the Tropic of Capricorn (23.5° S latitude).

The pattern of rising and falling air in the atmosphere shifts north and south with the sun, though usually lagging by a month or two. In winter, Crater Lake takes the westerlies full on and embraces storm after storm. In the summer, the westerlies shift to the north and track mostly into British Columbia. Crater Lake receives little rain at this time, and after the snowpack melts, the land becomes quite dry. Winter obviously presents plants with challenges, but summer does too. Plants on the porous pumice soil can find it difficult to secure enough moisture to survive, much less grow and bloom.

At the height of summer, the westerlies push far enough north that moist tropical air reaches southern Oregon from the south. The humid air boils up on hot days, forming thunderstorms. Sometimes Crater Lake endures drenching rains and always thunder and lightning. While not numerous, the storms can ignite fires that can burn large areas of forest. This natural process has repeated itself throughout time. The plants in the region are adapted to this cycle of burn and recover. The birds, too, have come to take advantage of this cycle.

Black-backed and American Three-toed Woodpeckers are some of the first to discover and colonize a burn, followed by ground foragers including Dark-eyed Juncos, American Robins, and bluebirds as the herbaceous vegetation recovers. Soon the appearance of woody vegetation draws others, and the cycle continues.

GEOLOGY AND ITS ROLE

Mount Mazama is part of the High Cascades, young by most geologic standards. The series of eruptions that resulted in 12,000-foot-tall Mount Mazama occurred just 70,000 to 420,000 years ago. The western foothills of the Cascades are much older (5–6 million years) but were created by the same process.

The surface of the earth is composed of eight major plates and numerous minor plates. These are quite thin relative to the earth. They are something like the "skin" that can form on top of hot chocolate. These solid plates cover the entire planet including the bottom of the ocean. They ride on the hot upper layer of the mantle. The upper mantle is not quite solid and not quite liquid, and it moves. The crustal plates float on top of this layer and are carried about. Sometimes they slide past each other. This process is anything but smooth, resulting in earthquakes. The San Andreas Fault marks the boundary of two crustal plates. California—the southwestern part of it at least—is sliding past the North American plate. Someday California could be a peninsula or island to the west of Oregon. When that happens, Oregon's climate will change, becoming much drier, as the westerlies will have to ascend one more set of mountains before reaching Crater Lake.

Sometimes plates move away from each other. As they do, lava quietly moves up to fill the gap. These are called spreading ridges. Iceland and a line down the center of the Atlantic Ocean is the best-known spreading ridge. Another is submerged just off the Oregon Coast.

Plates may also collide. When this happens, one plate usually rides up over the other, forming a set of mountains paralleling the collision. The North American Plate is moving west at a rate of 2.5 inches a year relative to the Juan de Fuca Plate, the small plate that forms the ocean bottom off the Oregon Coast. As the North American Plate moves west, the Juan de Fuca Plate is forced down into the mantle. This also takes place in sudden jumps as the plates stick and break free. Why Oregon and Washington don't experience large earthquakes more often is a question that entertains geologists. There should be more!

As the Juan de Fuca plate descends into the hot mantle, it begins to melt. This magma rises in "bubbles" or blobs toward the surface and typically pauses in a chamber some distance below the surface. Periodically some of this magma reaches the surface as lava flows or, sometimes explosively, creates volcanoes.

The magma residing in a chamber beneath the surface changes over time, and this alters the chemistry of the lava that reaches the surface. Initially, magma is a mix of iron- and magnesium-rich minerals, dark in color, combined with lighter-colored quartz, feldspars, and micas. The first lavas to reach the surface are basalts rich in the darker-colored minerals. These rocks form the base of the Cascade volcanoes. However, as the magma in the chamber deep beneath the surface begins to cool, minerals with the highest melting points begin to crystallize out. These include iron- and magnesium-containing minerals. Thus, over time, the erupting lavas become lighter in color as the darker minerals are left behind. This is why so many of the rocks found in the Cascades are gray. This gray rock is andesite, named for the Andes where the rock was described.

Eventually, the melted material remaining in the magma chamber is largely quartz. Eruptions of this material produce both pumice and obsidian. The difference is determined by the amount of moisture in the magma. If the magma is "dry," the lava simply cools into a glass we call obsidian. Obsidians are common in Newberry Crater to the northeast near Bend. However, if the magma contains sufficient moisture, the moisture vaporizes into countless steam bubbles when the pressure on the magma is released upon reaching the surface. The frothy lava solidifies into pumice before the bubbles of steam can escape. The magma in the eruption that resulted in the formation of Crater Lake was relatively rich in moisture.

Recent volcanic rocks, especially andesite and basalt, tend to be rich in the nutrients needed for plant growth. These nutrients are released as the rocks weather and erode. Pumice, in contrast, being largely quartz, produces less fertile soils.

When Mount Mazama erupted about 7700 years ago, the westerlies were blowing strong. Most of the pumice launched into the atmosphere drifted east and northeast, creating vast and deep pumice deposits. Pumice is quite porous, explaining why it floats in water. Pumice soils absorb considerable moisture, but they cannot hold on to it long. The porosity of the soils explains the scarcity of streams in the eastern and northeastern portions of the park. Precipitation soaks into the earth before it has a chance to flow downhill.

Many of the ridges in the western and southern portions of the park were spared, and it is here that the richest soils are found. As expected, this difference in soils leads to differences in the forest communities and the birds found in different parts of the park. For example, Sooty Grouse and White-crowned Sparrows are most abundant on the richer soils.

ELEVATION AND ITS ROLE

Geographic location and geology explain much about the climate and forest communities, but one additional factor needs to be considered— elevation. The relationship with precipitation patterns has already been explored, but elevation leads to other patterns as well. Elevations in the park range from about 4200' to 8929' (Mount Scott).

As a general rule, spring arrives one day later with every 100' increase in elevation. Similarly, fall begins one day earlier with every 100' increase in elevation. This can make for a very short growing season at higher elevations. Frosts can occur on almost any night. Snow may fall at any time. Plants and birds that cannot tolerate the cold and unpredictable weather at the higher elevations will be confined to lower elevations outside of the park where it is more benign.

Clark's Nutcrackers, Canada Jays, Gray-crowned Rosy-Finches, and American Pipits are some of the breeding birds found at higher elevations that are seldom encountered elsewhere.

Perhaps a more important consequence of elevation for birds is the effect on the food supply. Birds, being warm-blooded flying machines, demand high-energy food and lots of it. Green leafy vegetation is not adequate fare for birds, with few exceptions. Geese are some of the few salad-eating birds. Insects in contrast are an excellent source of energy. While it is possible to find spiders and insects on any day and in any place in the park, the numbers can be very small for much of the year. The population explosion of insects each year does not occur until bud-break. For conifers at the higher elevations, this might be July or even early August. Spring migration for many forest birds in Oregon occurs in late April and early May—the high-elevation forests are just not ready.

Consequently, many birds must seek out forests at lower elevations as a place to nest, and avoid the park.

Not all insects live in the canopy of forests. Woodpeckers have little trouble finding beetle larvae boring beneath the bark and through the wood of dead trees even in winter. Thus, it should come as no surprise that Crater Lake National Park is an excellent place to look for woodpeckers.

Seeds are another excellent source of energy, and elevation indirectly affects their availability. Seeds that fall to the ground are concealed by a blanket of snow for much of the year. Some conifers retain at least some of their seeds in the canopy, where they remain relatively free of snow. Several seed eating species of birds frequent the park in even the bitterest weather if the squirrels have not harvested all the cones.

Then there are the carnivores. Hawks and owls can persist through winter, though potential prey are fewer. Although owls and some diurnal raptors may be found throughout the winter, many depart to where there is less snow and prey is more plentiful and accessible.

HABITATS AND THEIR ROLE
Crater Lake

Crater Lake is a deep lake (1943 feet), the deepest in the United States and second only to Great Slave Lake in North America. The bottom plunges quickly from the shore into the abyss. Except for a limited area surrounding Wizard Island, there are no extensive shallows for the sun to warm the water and produce the rich broth of algae, diatoms, and the host of aquatic invertebrates that feed on them.

Residing in a caldera, Crater Lake has no great rivers or even modest streams supplying water to the lake. Snowmelt tumbles and cascades into the water of the lake, but it comes from no great distance and has little chance to accumulate and deliver nutrients from the soil or fallen leaves. Crater Lake is nutrient-poor. The term aquatic ecologists apply to such lakes is "oligotrophic," which means "little food." Researchers sometimes refer to Crater Lake as "ultraoligotrophic" to emphasize just how nutrient-poor it is. For this reason, Crater Lake has incredible clarity. There is little plankton to absorb light. It is a thin soup indeed.

Scientists monitor the clarity of Crater Lake and other bodies of water with a simple device called a Secchi disk—a disk 6 inches in diameter, like a pie cut into quarters. Two of the slices are painted black and two white. The Secchi disk is lowered into the lake until it can no longer be seen from the surface. The depth at which it disappears from sight provides a measure of clarity. A recent measure for Crater Lake is an amazing 142 feet, making it the clearest lake in the world, clearer than even Lake Tahoe.

It would be a mistake to conclude that there is no life in Crater Lake. A wide range of planktonic organisms and a host of aquatic insects call the lake home, although they are thinly spread. Aquatic mosses festoon the rocky sides down to an incredible depth of about 400 feet. This may not seem that deep, but in the ocean, it is black at these depths. No light penetrates to support any photosynthetic organisms. The plankton, what little there is in Crater Lake, tends to reside relatively deep.

Originally, there were no fish in the lake. The first introduction was made by William Steele in 1888. Crayfish were introduced soon after. An endemic form of rough-skinned newt (*Taricha granulosa*) would have been the largest aquatic animal patrolling the limited shallows. Spotted Sandpipers undoubtedly bobbed along the shoreline searching for insect prey. The addition of fish to the lake has brought about changes. Certainly, the plankton and aquatic invertebrate communities were markedly altered as they contended with new predators. However, the addition of kokanee salmon (*Oncorhynchus nerka*) and rainbow trout (*O. mykiss*) are probably responsible for the presence of Common Mergansers, a pair of Bald Eagles, and occasionally Osprey at the lake. In years of high fish availability, Double-crested Cormorants may breed.

Many migrant waterbirds pause to rest and feed a bit before moving on. The California Gull is the most frequent visitor, but during migration a variety of diving ducks, grebes, and phalaropes can sometimes be seen. While the waters of Crater Lake usually remain open throughout the winter, it is not a good time to be a bird on Crater Lake. Food is scarce and the winter winds blow cold.

Cliffs and Rocky Areas

The volcano is a layer cake of igneous rock consisting of alternating layers of andesite and cinders. The cinders were formed when eruptions launched molten material high into the air and the spray of lava cooled into ash, pumice, and cinders before landing. These rubble piles are loose and form little more than steep hillsides as erosion slowly dismantles the mountain. The andesite and dacite, which are much more durable, formed from the lava flows that were extruded from the mountain and flowed down its sides. As the mountain erodes, the andesite forms cliffs and rims, home to a select set of birds.

The cliffs themselves serve as nesting sites for the Peregrine Falcon and Common Raven. Other raptors such as Red-tailed Hawks, Northern Harriers, and Golden Eagles ride the winds that rise off the face as convenient places to fly when visiting. Rock Wrens are one of the most common inhabitants, occupying even the smallest rims that provide them with food, shelter, and nesting sites. Gray-crowned Rosy-Finches also dwell on the cliffs and talus slopes when not foraging on snowfields, and Violet-green Swallows patrol the steep slopes for flying insects.

Shrubland

Shrubland constitutes a rather limited habitat within the park and tends to occur on drier south-facing slopes such as those near the Pinnacles along Sun Creek and near the south boundary of the park. The dry shrubland in the park is dominated by snowbrush, green-leaf manzanita, and golden chinkapin (*Castanopsis castanea*) in areas of better developed soils and bitterbrush on the more recent pumice soils and where the snowpack is thinner. Shrubland also occurs in places inside the rim on the south-facing slopes.

Along the Cleetwood Trail, the green-leaf manzanita is the dominant shrub. These shrubs are evergreen, with tough leathery leaves that resist water loss. As resistant as they are to drought and extreme heat, they are sensitive to cold temperatures and survive only where the winter snow provides an insulating blanket. Under the snow, the temperature seldom drops more than a few degrees below the freezing point, often much warmer than the air above. The height of the shrubs at mid- and lower elevations can be a good indication of the average minimum snow depth in an area. In years of very low snowfall, the exposed portions of the shrubs may experience severe frost damage.

Shrubs respond more quickly after a fire than trees. Some, like the green-leaf manzanita, resprout almost immediately after a fire has passed through an area, while others germinate in profusion the spring following a fire, sprouting from a dormant seed bank that has accumulated in the soil. Shrubland is, perhaps, less abundant in the park than it was seventy years ago. This likely indicates that stand-replacing fires have not visited these areas in some time. Shrubland can still be found in the vicinity of the Panhandle and at the Pinnacles. For the adventurous, a trip down the dusty and rutted back roads bordering the eastern margin of the park will introduce you to more extensive shrubland of ceanothus and manzanita.

Shrubland is inhabited by a special set of bird species, many of which are found nowhere else in the park. Many of these species feed either among the low vegetation or among the leaf litter beneath. Many are ground nesters. Shrubland birds include Dusky Flycatchers, Nashville Warblers, Green-tailed Towhees, and Fox Sparrows.

Riparian

Riparian habitats are those that grow where streams and lakes provide an abundant and dependable supply of water to the roots of plants. Even on the hottest summer day you can feel the cool moist air in the shade of riparian plants. Dig your fingers into riparian soil and it will be moist and rich. Riparian habitats are typically rich in life, rich in productivity, and rich in species. At lower elevations, the plentiful water promotes a broad and dense zone of vegetation along the waterways including willows (*Salix* spp.), alders (*Alnus* spp.), and cottonwoods (*Populus trichocarpa*). Beneath these trees is often a layer of shorter shrubs, with a dense layer of herbaceous plants under that.

Riparian habitats along streams are prone to disturbance. Periodic floods and moving stream channels undercut streamside vegetation and remove stretches of trees and other vegetation. This renewal process creates open patches, clean gravel bars, back channels, and ponds, all a part of the riparian habitat necessary to maintain a healthy habitat with the resources to meet the needs of all the inhabitants. At higher elevations, where the conifers tower over a narrow stream and the stream is carved into a steep-walled valley, the zone may become a very narrow strip or even be absent.

Within the park, the riparian zone is not well represented. The high mountain streams on young volcanic soil offer limited opportunities for riparian habitat to develop. It is best developed around the wet meadows at high elevations and along the lower reaches of Annie and Sun Creeks.

More extensive riparian habitats exist to the south of the park, along the Wood River near Fort Klamath.

Lazuli Buntings, MacGillivray's Warblers, Lincoln's Sparrows, and White-crowned Sparrows live in the wet meadows with willow and alder. Dippers live on the upper reaches of the streams. All these plus Western Warbling Vireos, Swainson's Thrushes, Wilson's Warblers, and Song Sparrows occur farther down the watershed. White-crowned Sparrows are the exception, occurring only in the highest meadows.

Montane Meadows

The montane meadows in the park take on a very different character depending on the soil. On pumice soil, such as at the Pumice Desert to the north of the rim, the porous soils quickly dry after the snow melts away, creating a sudden burst of growth that quickly fades. Low-growing pussypaws (*Calyptridium umbellatum*) and knotweed (*Polygonum* sp.) are a couple of the most common plants. While the large open areas provide vistas of the other mountains in the Cascades, few birds inhabit these meadows except for a small population of Horned Larks on Llao Rock. Around the fringes of the meadows, Mountain Bluebirds, Chipping Sparrows, and Dark-eyed Juncos forage. In late summer and early fall these are joined by Red-tailed Hawks, American Pipits and White-crowned Sparrows.

On the southern and western slopes of the mountain, such as at Munson Meadows, the soil is more productive, retaining soil moisture long after the snow has melted. These meadows support a luxuriant growth of flowers including Jacob's ladder (*Polemonium californicum*), Indian paintbrush (*Castilleja* spp.), larkspur (*Delphinium nuttallianum*), columbine (*Aquilegia formosa*), cow parsnip (*Heracleum maximum*), lupine (*Lupinus* spp.), and a host of others. The meadows are interspersed with small islands of true fir and mountain hemlock. In places springs emerge from the hillside to feed the growing streams that tumble down the sides of the mountain often buried in short willows, thin-leaf alder (*Alnus incana*), and mountain ash (*Sorbus sitchensis*). The late snowmelt in these areas keeps trees from invading the meadows.

In late summer hummingbirds become quite common as flowers at lower elevations become scarce. You will find Rufous Hummingbirds and a few Calliope and Black-chinned Hummingbirds as they prepare

Llao Rock

for the fall migration. In the wet meadows you can find nesting MacGilli-vray's Warblers, Lincoln's Sparrows, and White-crowned Sparrows. Late summer brings a number of migrants to feed on the abundance of insects and seeds.

Forest Communities

It is convenient to speak of the different forest communities as if they were discrete entities. For the most part, however, they are not. The mix of species changes continuously with changes in the environment, depending on the combination of physical and biological factors required by each species. From lowest to highest elevation, the dominant trees on the western slopes change from Douglas-fir to white fir to mountain hem-lock and Shasta fir (*A. magnifica* x *A. procera*) and eventually to whitebark pine. At the lower elevations, the primary change involves Douglas-fir on the moister sites giving way to ponderosa pine on the drier sites on the eastern slopes. In each case sharp divisions are seldom between the ranges of species. One species gradually become more common as conditions are more favorable while another declines in abundance.

However, sharp divisions between communities can be commonly observed in two situations. The first involves disturbance, such as fire. Lodgepole pines (*P. contorta*) are admirably adapted to colonize recently cleared areas. It is often possible to determine the margins of a stand-replacing fire decades later by following the boundary between a nearly pure stand of lodgepole pine on one side and the adjacent forest composed of a mix of different species on the other.

The second situation wherein a more or less clear division occurs between forest communities is the average limit of the snowpack. Each winter at higher elevations snow accumulates on the forest floor and remains until spring melt. At lower elevations, snow may fall, but it seldom remains long, melting out between storms. The areas where a snowpack develops are relatively consistent from year to year, and this shapes forest communities. In southern Oregon this typically occurs between 3500' and 4500' depending on aspect, lower on north- and east-facing slopes and higher on south- and west-facing slopes. White fir as well as other true firs and mountain hemlock are dominant where a snowpack develops.

You can easily assess the average depth of the snowpack in an area dominated by white fir by looking for the bright yellow-green wolf lichens (*Letharia vulpina*) growing on the trunks of the trees. The lichens do not grow on the portions of the trunk regularly covered by snow in winter.

Douglas-fir, in contrast, becomes dominant at lower elevations where snow does not accumulate. It is unclear whether Douglas-fir cannot tolerate a snowpack or whether white fir is competitively dominant in areas with a snowpack.

The forests of southern Oregon are diverse, and it helps to understand the ecology of the area if we speak of "communities." Keep in mind the limitations of the community concept as you read about the following forest types.

LODGEPOLE PINE. The lodgepole pine forest is not diverse. Three species tend to dominate, one tree, one shrub, and one grass. In addition to the lodgepole pine, the shrub is bitterbrush and the grass is Idaho fescue. Of course, other species of plants exist there, but as you drive down the road through a lodgepole pine forest, these three may be the only species you notice.

Wizard Island

Lodgepole pines are largely restricted to porous and nutrient-poor soils. They have extensive and deep roots that seek out the seasonally scarce water in the soil. They also appear to be poor competitors. On richer soils, other species such as ponderosa pine and true firs crowd them out. However, the pumice soils suit them well, and the extensive plains of Mazama ash surrounding Crater Lake provide a spacious home.

It has been 7700 years since Mount Mazama buried much of the landscape in pumice and ash. The rule of thumb in ecology is that it takes 500 years to produce an inch of soil. Even taking into consideration that everything takes longer at high elevations, there should be somewhere between six inches and a foot of soil. Yet a stroll through a lodgepole pine forest reveals a thin and very patchy covering of fallen needles, nothing resembling the rich, aromatic soils teeming with worms, millipedes, and other organisms found elsewhere. Mostly it is mineral soil—in other words, pumice. Where is the soil?

Scientists have discovered a fascinating cycle involving fire, beetles, and lodgepole pine that has been repeated a great many times since the pumice and ash was deposited. Let us begin with bare pumice following a fire. Seeds that have lain dormant in the soil, often for many years, sprout as the snows melt in the spring. Each year the pines grow, adding a whorl of new limbs and 2–12 inches of height depending on the growing conditions. When only a few years old, the trees begin to produce small cones about 2 inches in diameter. In the Rocky Mountains and some other areas, the cones hold on tight to the seeds, the bracts sealed with resin. The seeds within retain viability for a great many years, longer than the seeds of most plants. Fire melts the resin and releases the seeds. In the Cascades, the lodgepole pines release their seeds at maturity and the seeds scatter, with many scuffed into the loose soil. Like its Rocky Mountain cousins, the seeds remain viable for many years, waiting. Squirrels, chipmunks, mice, and jays take their percentage, but a great many escape detection.

As the tree grows, other organisms see the tree as a source of food. One in particular is important to this ecological story, the mountain pine beetle (*Dendroctonus ponderosae*). An adult male beetle will bore into the bark of a pine in hopes of attracting a mate and laying eggs. The gallery he creates runs horizontally under the bark. If all goes well for the beetle, the eggs will hatch, and the larvae will eat their way through the tender cambium layer that is vital to the tree. The resulting pattern left behind in the bark and surface of the wood is distinctive. The horizontal gallery created by the adults is a few inches long and relatively large in diameter. The tiny galleries formed by the hundred or so larvae fan out upward and downward from the central gallery, increasing in size as the larvae grow; the resulting pattern is reminiscent of a long-legged centipede. Too many larvae and the tree is in peril. However, if the tree is healthy and the infestation is light, it can usually repel the beetles by exuding sap and forcing the beetle to leave. Even more important than the tree's defenses is the winter weather. When a tree is small, the bark is thin. It provides little protection from the cold and bitter winter weather, and beetle larvae in these trees usually die. By the time dense stands of lodgepole pine attain 80–100 years of age, the bark becomes thick enough to offer beetle larvae a measure of protection against bitter winter temperatures. Mild winters further enhance larval survival. Low soil moisture from drought is an additional factor that impairs the tree's ability to fend off the beetles.

When the combination of bark thickness, winter temperatures, and soil moisture conspire to permit high larval survival, the bark beetle nuisance can become a major outbreak. The trees are not able to resist the overwhelming numbers, and vast stands of pines die. The last time this happened in the Crater Lake area was in the early 2000s. Between Bend and Klamath Falls, great swaths of land were reduced to barren dead trees. In the centuries before Smokey the Bear, these extensive stands of dead pines stood until a summer thunderstorm touched off the tinder dry trees with a bolt of lightning. The resulting fire cleansed the landscape. The trees burned, and the accumulating litter and fallen wood burned, restoring the soil to barren pumice. The seeds long waiting beneath the surface, awakened by the heat, germinated in profusion the following spring to begin the 80–100 year cycle once again.

Without the beetles, fires would be less extensive and less intense, and organic matter would accumulate on the ground over time. The resulting enriched soils would eventually become capable of supporting ponderosa pine and additional plants. These would crowd out the lodgepole pine until the next volcanic eruption or chance intense fire created open space for lodgepole pines to colonize. As it is, the soil supports limited productivity and relatively little food for bird populations. Further, green pine needles tend to support only a modest grazing invertebrate population, again limiting opportunities for birds.

Characteristic birds of this habitat include Steller's Jays, Common Ravens, Mountain Chickadees, Western Tanagers, Yellow-rumped Warblers, Dark-eyed Juncos, Red Crossbills, and, though sparse, several woodpeckers, including Northern Flickers, Hairy Woodpeckers, Black-backed Woodpeckers, and American Three-toed Woodpeckers.

PONDEROSA PINE. Except for the western juniper (*Juniperus occidentalis*), ponderosa pine is the most drought-tolerant conifer in Oregon. Traveling east down the slopes of the Cascades and into the high desert, we encounter less and less precipitation, and it becomes warmer. One tree after another finds life too challenging and drops out. First it is the true firs, then the Douglas-fir. Finally, the ponderosa pine yields to the juniper and sage when the annual precipitation falls below about 15 inches.

At Crater Lake, ponderosas are most common along the southern and eastern boundaries of the park. With time trees lose the dark brown bark typical of younger trees, and the bark becomes yellow to rich orange. This gives rise to several popular names for this species including "yellow pine" and "yellow bellies." Their bark is unique in other ways as well. Approach one closely and you will see the small irregular plates that make up the bark. This is why ponderosas are called "puzzle-bark" trees by some. From a distance, ponderosas often look like they are growing from a small hill. The hill is formed from shed pieces of bark.

Ponderosa pines tolerate fire quite well. Their bark is thick and fire resistant. Most of the older trees show charring and fire scars where they have survived past burns.

The wood of ponderosa pine is sought after commercially for appearance, but it is relatively soft and unsuitable for most structural applications. However, soft wood is ideal for woodpeckers and other excavators that nest and roost in cavities. Ponderosas teem with woodpeckers and nuthatches.

Old-growth ponderosa pine forests are home to many threatened bird species and species of concern including American Goshawk, Flammulated Owl, Great Gray Owl, White-headed Woodpecker, Williamson's Sapsucker, and Pygmy Nuthatch. Other birds common in the ponderosa pine forests include Mountain Chickadees, Townsend's Solitaires, Western Tanagers, Yellow-rumped Warblers, Dark-eyed Juncos, Red Crossbills, and Cassin's Finches.

WHITE FIR. As you climb the winding roads into the Cascades, at some point the forest changes rather abruptly. Instead of Douglas-fir and a mixture of other species in the west, or ponderosa pine in the east, you enter a forest of white fir. Scattered western white pines grow among the firs but little else. As explained above, the change occurs as soon as you reach the area where a regular snowpack accumulates each winter.

White fir is a dominant tree at lower elevations in Crater Lake National Park. It is a tall tree regularly exceeding 120 feet in height but does not rival the Douglas-fir. The foliage is dense, and the sprays of needles have a more rounded appearance than the more pointed branches of the Douglas-fir. The cones are concentrated near the tops of the trees and stand erect until they disintegrate, dispersing their seeds.

White fir occurs in the densest stands between 4000 and 6000 feet elevation everywhere except on new pumice soils. White fir grows densely with a closed canopy that permits little light to penetrate to the forest floor. Fallen needles accumulate over many years, often forming a spongy mat laced with the mycelium of fungi. Where many conifers self-prune, white firs tend to retain their lower limbs except in the densest of stands. A thin carpet of perennial plants that can tolerate the deep shade provides some green including anemones (*Anemone* sp.), synthyris (*Synthyris* sp.), and calypso orchids (*Calypso bulbosa*).

White firs are prone to heart rot. You may see weeping catfaces (draining scars) where an injury has permitted the entry of bacteria and fungus. Carpenter ants (*Camponotus* sp.) are quick to find this softened wood and establish large colonies within the trunks of these trees. Pileated Woodpeckers specialize on these ants and are common in this forest. Other common birds include the Hairy Woodpecker, Hammond's Flycatcher, Golden-crowned Kinglet, Brown Creeper, Red-breasted Nuthatch, Hermit Thrush, Yellow-rumped Warbler, Hermit Warbler, and Dark-eyed Junco.

MOUNTAIN HEMLOCK/SHASTA FIR. The forests at the highest elevations in the Oregon Cascades, before giving way to the meadows at timberline, are composed of mountain hemlock and Shasta fir. Only whitebark pine and subalpine fir occur higher on the exposed windblown ridges. Mountain hemlock, like its lowland relative, the western hemlock (*Tsuga heterophylla*) grows with a droopy top. It makes identification easy from a distance. Its seeds are tiny, and its cones are small. The bluish needles tightly wrapped around the stems of the Shasta fir are distinctive. The cones are large, but like those of all true firs, the cones disintegrate at maturity releasing the seeds.

Trees here must contend with a short growing season, heavy snow, and high winds. The trees have limber and resilient limbs to permit snow to slough off before acquiring so much weight that limbs break. They also are narrow trees with short limbs for the same reason. Like an A-frame structure, narrow trees shed snow easily.

Trees may be far older than they appear in this habitat, for the growing season is short and growth is slow. Trees 4 inches in diameter may be more than 100 years old. Bud break typically occurs in July or early

August, providing just enough time for a few inches of growth before fall arrives in the high country.

The insects that live here tend to be small, in part so they can complete their life cycle in the brief time that the growing conditions are suitable. The birds also tend to be small. No grosbeaks or vireos and relatively few tanagers breed here, though they may visit in migration. The most common species in this habitat are Golden-crowned Kinglets, Mountain Chickadees, Yellow-rumped Warblers, Dark-eyed Juncos, Pine Siskins, and Cassin's Finches.

WHITEBARK PINE. The great forests of the Pacific Northwest teem with trees of incredible size. They also harbor a great number of conifer species, a number unmatched anywhere else in the world. Crater Lake National Park is no exception. The tiny island called Phantom Ship alone sustains eight different species of conifers. However, one species merits special distinction, the whitebark pine. It persists on the highest ridges, often above the mountain hemlock, where it must endure the rigors of winter. On these exposed ridges it must withstand the full force of winter storms, finding little shelter from the biting wind that whips abrasive ice particles off the slopes and slams them against the trunk, needles, and vulnerable buds with an effect much like a sandblaster. It is a tough tree that can survive such abuse.

Because whitebark pines grow in such inaccessible places, and seldom in abundance, relatively few people have seen the cones of this tree. They are the size of a fist and more or less round. Their bracts shelter large and nutritious seeds. Such an important source of food in this impoverished landscape does not go unnoticed. In the Greater Yellowstone ecosystem, grizzly bear (*Ursus arctos*) depend heavily on the seeds from this tree as a late summer food to sustain them through winter's hibernation. Grizzlies once roamed the slopes of the Cascades. One of the last, named Reelfoot, was killed south of the park near Pilot Rock in 1890. It is likely that they once regularly visited the rim of Crater Lake in late summer and early fall in search of whitebark pinecones.

While not as imposing, one bird relies heavily on the seeds from this tree, the Clark's Nutcracker. More likely than not, you will hear them as you step from your vehicle at the rim of Crater Lake. This bird can live in this hostile environment even during the winter when most other birds have long since retreated to points south or at least to lower elevations.

BY THE SEASONS
Early Spring: Awakenings

It is April. In the valleys west of the Cascades the daffodils have come and gone, and the cottonwoods are in full leaf, fluttering in the breezes of a cool spring evening. Flowers are abundant, and the oak woodland wears many colors. Certainly, there are frosts yet to come, as well as late storms, but spring is in full force. Birds that wintered in Mexico and other points south are rushing north, with new species arriving every day. The Violet-green and Tree Swallows are already building nests, having returned in February and early March. Mid-April is a wonderful time in southern Oregon at the lower elevations.

Up on the rim of Crater Lake is a different story. From the valley floor, the volcanic peaks of the high Cascades shine white. This is the promise of water that will fill the rivers through the summer, supporting salmon, mergansers, and farmers. Depending on the year, 8, 10, maybe 20 feet of snow still cover the rim. The sun is warming, but there is still a bite in the air in the shadows. The last snowstorms have yet to add their modest contribution to the winter blanket of snow.

Still, the first signs of spring are unmistakable in the high country. You won't see it in spring wildflowers. The ground is still buried deep. Mountain hemlock and Shasta fir are still deep in winter sleep. It will be months before buds begin to swell. The snow is thinning rapidly in the Panhandle at the lowest elevation in the park, at around 4000 feet, where there is bare ground and the first green shoots are pushing through the carpet of pine needles. Willows and alders in the deep canyon along Annie Creek are just beginning to bloom. The catkins add their pollen to the air even though the flowers lack colorful petals. The shade of the canyon and the cool air sliding down the canyon from the snowfields higher up will keep the new leaves tightly wrapped in their buds for a while longer.

Although the Canada Jays and a few other birds rode out the winter in the park, their numbers were sparse. Mid-April brings new arrivals to the high country. One of the first to arrive is the Dark-eyed Junco. Their trill can be heard at the lower elevation in the park, but near the rim they feed quietly for a bit longer. The food resources must be few, considering that juncos are ground foragers. There must be just enough conifer seeds and numbed insects on the retreating snow to sustain them, emphasizing how vital it must be to arrive early to claim one of the better territories before others beat them to it. It is the promise of better days ahead that brings them to the park before winter releases its grip.

Yellow-rumped Warblers also arrive at this time. Their morning songs compete with the sound of the breezes in the ponderosa pines. Still, it is early in the season, and the bout of singing is brief. Females are prudently waiting another week or two before arriving. Yellow-rumped Warblers precede most other species of warblers in the spring migration. The bold white, black, and yellow markings add a touch of color to the landscape.

Another of the early migrants is the Red-breasted Sapsucker. The bright carmine red heads almost glow against a background of white snow and deep blue skies. The silent contests among males for choice territories and the competition for mates is already under way. Birds chase one another among the tall firs. What food the sapsuckers manage to find at this time is also a puzzle. The sap in the trees is not abundant, and the insects that supplement their diet have yet to awaken. The early days of spring are challenging.

The arrival of the full complement of breeding species is still weeks away, awaiting more favorable conditions both in warming temperatures as well as the promise of abundant food. It will be June before all are here, racing the clock to produce a new crop of young before the first snows bring the brief summer to an end.

Summer: Solstice

Summer solstice—the longest day of the year and the shortest night. The date signals the beginning of the end for spring in the valleys below. The oppressive heat is settling in weeks at a time on the valley floor. There have already been many days in the 90s. Days reaching 100°F by the solstice are not rare. Most of the annual plants in the savannas and along the roadsides have withered in the parched soils, leaving their seeds to wait for the next growing season. Many of the perennials have also gone into dormancy, waiting patiently for the fall rains to begin to replenish the moisture in the soil.

By late June, singing is starting to abate. The breeding season is beginning to wrap up. The young of many species have fledged. Young robins with spotted breasts work the lawns and pastures like seasoned pros, and young geese are nearing the size of their parents. Young chickadees, titmice, and nuthatches have been out and about for more than a month, and the young, having acquired the necessary survival skills, have begun to disperse. Others are feeding ravenous nestlings nearing the point of fledging.

The story is different in the high country above 6000 feet. Spring is just arriving. Snow fields are still retreating, followed closely by the perennials emerging from the newly exposed earth. The plants are in a hurry to complete a season's growth before the snow returns. The candles (buds) of the lodgepole pines are just beginning to lengthen, giving hint to just how much growth can be expected this year. Except in the warmest locations, the mountain hemlock and true fir are not yet even swelling in the bud. They are still waiting. Without new growth there is little for insects to feed on. With few insects, rearing a family of young birds is a daunting task at best. Patience.

Still, there are those that manage despite the challenges. At high elevations there are limits to the luxury of patience. The summer season is short. Canada Jays are the first to fledge. The young wear a uniform, charcoal gray in contrast to the gray, white, and dark brown pattern of the adults. Young silently trail after the parents as they scour the forest for anything edible. The Canada Jays succeed, in part, because they have been preparing for the breeding season for some time. As discussed elsewhere, they cache food that not only sustains them through the winter but also serves to help rear young before food becomes plentiful.

Others also push hard on the early season. Within a few days of the solstice short-tailed Dark-eyed Juncos will fledge and follow parents among the sparse carpet of white-veined pyrola (*Pyrola picta*) and mountain gooseberry (*Ribes montigenum*) growing in the shade of the conifers. Apparently, foraging on the ground provides opportunities sooner than for those looking for insects in the canopy.

Others will follow soon. The young Hairy Woodpeckers are growing fast, and the parents work hard to satisfy the growing brood.

Many of the insect-eating birds at higher elevations must wait. The table has yet to be set. Yellow-rumped Warblers lag behind their relatives at lower elevations in the park by two weeks or more, even though they add ground foraging and flycatching to their search strategy. Hermit Warblers nesting above 4000 feet may wait until July to get serious about breeding. It is not uncommon to see recently fledged young chasing after parents begging for one more caterpillar in the third and fourth weeks of August.

In the valleys, from April through June a chaotic burst of birdsong greets the brightening sky in the east beginning about 45 minutes before sunrise. This is the dawn chorus. It starts slowly with an American Robin or Hermit Thrush and then quickly explodes into a cacophony of song as other species join the chorus making it nearly impossible to isolate an individual singer. It ends abruptly as the sun's rays light up the treetops. Time to eat. After about an hour of feeding, many birds resume singing but without the intensity of the dawn chorus. Singing takes energy, and energy debts must be repaid.

At the solstice in the high country, the dawn chorus pales in comparison with the valley symphony. Above 6000 feet, at best, Yellow-rumped Warblers and Dark-eyed Juncos provide songs worthy enough to give reason to arise before dawn, for me at least. Even those birds that do sing do not appear to be committed to the effort. Bouts are short, with much pause between. The occasional Townsend's Solitaire or Cassin's Finch adds its voice, but nothing sustained. There is little energy in the dawn chorus because there is little energy to spare.

As evening approaches in the valleys below, there is often a modest rebound in singing. Warblers, tanagers, and especially the thrushes tune up for a last chorus before nightfall. The pace of singing is lethargic. One by one each species falls out of the chorus until the last, usually a thrush, brings the concert to a close.

An evening concert in the high county? Don't count on it. Only the Junco and Yellow-rumped Warbler and maybe a Hermit Thrush contribute the occasional song before darkness. It cannot be considered a concert by any definition.

Late Summer/Fall: A Northwest Roadhouse

In the outback of Australia, the distance between towns is often great. In between are kilometers upon kilometers of mulga, spinifex, mallee, and other sun-baked plants, home to a few but inhospitable to most. Along the highways and other principal routes of travel in this vast country, a few enterprising people have built roadhouses. These friendly waystations provide gas, food, lodging, and conversation to sustain travelers. This also fairly describes Crater Lake National Park in the summer and early autumn with respect to migratory birds.

In contrast with the forests in the foothills of the Cascades, along the rivers and streams of the lowlands, and in fields and brushlands, Crater Lake National Park is not a cradle for a great many birds. However, Crater Lake National Park provides an important service to many of the birds that raise their young in other areas. The High Cascades, including Crater Lake National Park, serve as roadhouses for birds that nest at lower elevations and eventually head for Mexico and other points south.

Spring comes late to the high country. Wildflowers bloom in profusion on the better soils of the park beginning in early July. Budbreak in the conifers comes in mid-July or even as late as early August, depending on the year. Although conifers retain needles year-round, a great many insects that feed on the foliage find them unpalatable once they finish growing and harden off. Given the toxic terpenes that permeate the mature needles and give conifers their "Christmas tree" smell, one might as well chew on cardboard soaked in turpentine. For much of the year, the insects that feed in the forest canopy are relatively few and small. Tiny bark lice (*Psocoptera*) are one of the most common; they feed mostly on the lichens that live on the trees. These tiny insects look like aphids but have chewing mouth parts instead of piercing and sucking mouth parts. The next most common group is the spiders. Add eggs, pupa, and the insects reared elsewhere in the forest that rest within the conifers and you have a thin gruel to sustain a modest population of insectivorous birds throughout much of the year.

Budbreak offers a strikingly different situation. The tender new growth of pines and other conifers is quite palatable to many grazing insects, especially lepidopteran caterpillars and sawfly larvae. In those relatively few weeks between budbreak and maturity of the needles, a host of hungry insects proliferates and take a share of the bounty. At a time when forests at lower elevations have largely completed their growth and are entering a relatively quiet phase as the drought of summer settles in, the high country provides rich opportunities for a variety of birdlife.

Below 4000 feet, the young of migratory birds begin to fill the forest as they fledge and begin to sharpen their foraging skills in late June and July. This is also the time the adults begin their molt in preparation for the long southward migration. It is the time of year that birds, both young and old, find the greatest need for the most energy. Many drift up into the high country. Here they share in the abundance, completing their preparations for the rigors of migration. These include Orange-crowned Warblers, Nashville Warblers, Black-throated Gray Warblers, Hermit Warblers, Townsend's Warblers, MacGillivray's Warblers, Black-headed Grosbeaks, Western Tanagers, Cassin's Vireos, White-crowned Sparrows, Lincoln's Sparrows, Green-tailed Towhees, and many more. They won't be announcing their presence with song, but if you are attentive, you will hear the quiet call notes that help to keep the loose flocks together as they scour the foliage in the forests and shrub fields. Once the young are experienced in the art of locating insects among the foliage and once the adults are clothed in a new set of feathers and laden with a layer of sustaining fat, they depart on the next leg of the journey south. The major movement occurs from mid-August on through September. By the frosts of early October, the forests of the high country are quiet once again, inhabited by little more than the faithful Mountain Chickadees, Red-breasted Nuthatches, Brown Creepers, and Golden-crowned Kinglets that worry the foliage until the next burst of spring bounty the following year.

Raptors, too, find the accommodations to their liking at their northwest roadhouse. In the high desert to the east of the Cascades, Belding's ground squirrels (*Urocitellus beldingi*) are one of their most important sources of food. However, by July all but the last of the young squirrels have put on enough fat to enter an eight-month rest. In winter scientists call the profound sleep hibernation. In summer they call it estivation. Ground squirrels estivate in July and roll it right into hibernation until about February, when the new plant growth among the sage is ready for them. Red-tailed Hawks, Prairie Falcons, and sometimes Swainson's and Ferruginous Hawks find the western pocket gophers (*Thomomys mazama*), golden-mantled ground squirrels (*Callospermophilus lateralis*), and chipmunks (*Tamias* sp.) along the crest of the Cascades to be the best fare around and often pause here before heading south.

The Cascades, with numerous high points and ridges to generate rising thermals of air and ridges to deflect the wind upward, make an ideal place to migrate with minimal effort. Beginning in early August and continuing well into October, watch for the steady stream of hawks effortlessly making their way south along this highway.

Winter: Endurance

Winter comes early to the high country and is reluctant to leave. The silence rings in the ears as a blanket of snow clinging to the drooping branches and covering the forest floor absorbs sounds before traveling a hundred yards. The forest feels abandoned for much of the year, but if you are patient and endure cold fingers and nose, you will be surprised at the array of life that makes its way through the leanest of times.

Put on a pair of snowshoes or cross-country skis and head out for a day's outing around the rim between storms, and you are likely to find not only the ever-present Common Raven playing in the wind but also curious Clark's Nutcrackers and Canada Jays. If you listen carefully, you might locate a family group or two of Mountain Chickadees, often in partnership with a few Red-breasted Nuthatches.

A great many birds have departed, some to Mexico, others farther. Many more have drifted down the mountainside to lower elevations, where the wind isn't as cutting and the snow doesn't accumulate. Hibernation is an option for some mammals, but only a single bird in the entire world is known to hibernate, the Common Poorwill. Poorwills are rare in the park. Other birds have found alternative ways to endure and remain active through the winter.

Although the opportunities to find food are fewer in winter, a living can still be earned, and some choose to remain. The first thing to appreciate is that the entire forest is not covered in snow. Yes, the forest floor is buried deep, and the trees are cloaked in a white mantle. For some mammals, such as red-backed voles (*Myodes californicus*) and western pocket gophers, this is a season relatively free from predation as they go about their activities beneath the snow. The only bird to join them is the Sooty Grouse. At night they roost in the interior of a tree beneath the mantle of snow. The snow may not exactly be warm, but there is much air trapped between the flakes, making it an effective insulator. Though the outside temperature may drop below zero and the winds blow, temperatures beneath the snow may not be much below freezing. Sooty Grouse feed largely on the buds of conifers in winter. As such, Sooty Grouse seldom have to leave a snow-covered tree. A flock can be in an area for months without betraying their presence with tracks in the snow.

Despite the snow, the trunks of the trees remain relatively unaffected, and a variety of birds take advantage of this snow-free space. Red-breasted Nuthatches scour the trunk and limbs for insect eggs, pupae, chilled insects, and seeds. Their trademark foraging style is to use their oversized feet to cling to the bark while moving headfirst down the trunk. By peering into cracks and crevices from above, they find food not visible to other bark-foraging birds.

Brown Creepers are the ecological complement of the Red-breasted Nuthatch. They forage on trunks in a manner different from the Red-breasted Nuthatch. Their strategy is to fly to the base of a tree and then spiral up, seeking invertebrates visible from below. Their long, thin beak is ideal for extracting prey from deep crevices.

Mountain Chickadees also scour the trunks of trees, but in addition they search branches and needles beneath the snow covering each limb. This provides them a secure space to forage, protected from both the biting winds and the eyes of predators.

The Golden-crowned Kinglet is the final member of this exclusive winter club of gleaners. It seldom seeks prey on the trunks of trees but moves in and among the snow-free portions of the branches and foliage, sharing the space with the Mountain Chickadees but feeding closer to the tips of the branches on average. They often hover in front of the tip of a branch seeking insects hidden among the buds, though not so much in the winter.

Woodpeckers, too, find winter to be no great obstacle. While they are content to glean insects from the snow-free trunks of trees, they also exploit the prey found beneath the bark in typical woodpecker fashion. The most common is the Hairy Woodpecker, but Black-backed and Three-toed Woodpeckers are also found in the lodgepole pine forests.

This suite of species often travels in loose flocks during the winter months, remaining in contact with one another with soft call notes. Families of chickadees and kinglets typically form the core of these foraging groups. One or a few nuthatches, creepers, and woodpeckers tag along, finding greater security with the many eyes keeping watch for predators. Such flocks often consist of a half dozen to more than fifty individuals.

Other inhabitants occupy the winter forest and forest edge. Canada Jays patrol the forest in family groups, alert for any potential source of food. Seeds and insects are always welcome, but the crack and crash of a falling tree often signals new opportunities and must be investigated. A winter-killed deer provides a wealth of food, often shared with other scavengers including Common Ravens and coyotes. Canada Jays have other tricks as well. They cache food for the lean times like their relative, the Clark's Nutcracker. However, they do it in their own fashion. They are "scatter hoarders," meaning they sequester a seed here or a dried insect in another crevice, and still some other morsel somewhere else. Their efforts are aided by sticky saliva that secures the food in place. A few Steller's Jays remain to face the winter with the Canada Jays, but many retreat to lower elevations. Steller's Jays are also known to cache food, but their dedication is no match for the Canada Jay or Nutcracker.

Though seldom encountered, predatory birds also remain in the park throughout the winter. The Great Gray Owl is a huge owl with a satellite dish for a face decorated with a white bow tie of feathers. The facial disc aids in gathering minute sounds beneath the snow. A mouse or gopher that feels secure in its maze of snow tunnels may not be as safe as it hopes. As it scurries along its tunnels or chews on some morsel, it cannot help but make some sound. Still, they are relatively safe deep beneath a foot or more of snow. However, snow tunnels tend to become depleted in oxygen, and mice must come near the surface on occasion where oxygen is more plentiful. It is here that the slight sounds make them vulnerable. The Great Gray Owl is listening. When snow blankets the area, they regularly plunge through the snow to capture the source of the sound. Northern Saw-whet Owls and American Goshawks are two other predatory birds that ride out the winter in the high country.

The streams house one special bird even in winter. Rapidly moving water is reluctant to freeze. Though snow may encroach on streams from the banks, and the stones and rocks that rise above the surface of the streams may be ringed in ice, the stream flows on in its quest for the ocean. Even near freezing, the waters harbor some of the richest food anywhere in the park in midwinter. The aquatic invertebrates continue with life as usual. So too, the American Dipper continues to forage even though the forest is carpeted in white. This uniformly dark bird with the short upright tail can be seen flying up and down the streams at any time of the year.

CLARK'S NUTCRACKER AND WHITEBARK PINE: A HIGH COUNTRY PARTNERSHIP

In his book *A Sand County Almanac*, Aldo Leopold wrote of the "numenon" of an area, the essence, that one species that embodies the spirit of a habitat. For the woodlots of Wisconsin, Aldo Leopold identified the Ruffed Grouse as the numenon. A copse that lacked its Ruffed Grouse was just a collection of trees. It is missing something vital and essential. Without the possibility of a grouse erupting from underfoot, a woodlot offers a pleasant walk but the excursion is incomplete, failing in some critical way to capture the imagination and provide a fulfilling experience.

At Crater Lake, the unquestioned numenon is the Clark's Nutcracker. Crater Lake without its Clark's Nutcrackers would still offer an unparalleled panorama, but you would be one step removed from the mountain experience. Here the Nutcracker has a special relationship with whitebark pine. Whitebark pines do not grow in large continuous stands, as do many other forest trees. Instead, whitebark pine clings to knife-edged ridges above timberline, in small groves or alone, toughing out the winter winds that hurls ice particles at the trunks and foliage. Before the winter winds arrive, they may produce a cone crop.

The fist-sized cones contain large seeds that, unlike other conifer seeds, bear no wing to help them disperse on the wind. Further, the cones can be opened easily, in sharp contrast to other pines, whose tough bracts tightly protect the contents. The pines have arrived at a different strategy for dispersing their seeds. They have come to rely on others, especially Clark's Nutcrackers, to carry off their seeds and plant them.

Clark's Nutcrackers prepare for the long year between cone crops from October through July by hiding whitebark pine seeds by the thousands. They dismantle the cones and tuck the seeds in a pouch beneath their tongue. Then off they fly to a chosen area that may be as little as 100 yards away or more than 20 miles. These areas are often selected because they are at lower elevations and winter winds keep the area from being

Clark's Nutcracker

buried deep in snow, leaving them accessible to the birds. They bury the seeds in the soil individually or in clusters of up to fifteen seeds.

Many animals cache food, but Clark's Nutcrackers are remarkable in their capacity to remember where they hid each cache of seeds even after many months have passed and after a layer of snow has changed the appearance of the landscape. The long-term spatial memory of the Clark's Nutcracker is unequalled among birds. Scientists have shown that they can remember the locations of more than 10,000 seeds for nearly a year, more than enough time to see them through the winter in style and even help feed a demanding brood of young in the spring. The region of the brain responsible for spatial memory in birds, and mammals as well, is called the hippocampus and is especially large in this species.

It should not be surprising that Nutcrackers display such intelligence. They are members of the crow, raven, magpie, and jay family, a group noted for its intellectual talents. Not only do they excel at spatial memory, but many species in the family also show aptitude in insight learning, problem solving skills, and even tool use.

Whitebark pine also benefits from this association with the Clark's Nutcracker. Having given up other traditional methods of dispersal, they depend on the Nutcracker to disperse their seeds. As good as the memory of the Nutcracker is, they still leave many seeds behind that germinate and produce new whitebark pines.

LIFE ON PUMICE SOILS

It takes special plants to endure on pumice soils, and the plants that do manage a living here grow slowly. Easily available water is present for only a short time each year, and soils are coarse, with much space between the grains, and contain little organic material. Thus, water percolates easily through these soils. Rain and melt water sink quickly beneath the surface, and because of this, streams are rare on pumice soils. Much of the water continues downward, far beyond the deepest roots. Being made of pumice, the larger particles are permeated by pores, bubbles of steam frozen in the cooling lava. These pores create more surface area on which a film of water adheres. This feature is important to the plants that grow here, but it is not enough. The water is soon depleted. There is just not enough surface area or organic matter in the soil to hold a reservoir of moisture to sustain plants over an extended growing season.

Soil nutrients are also scarce. Pumice consists of foamy quartz and maybe feldspars but little else. As it weathers, few nutrients are released to the developing soils. Between the lack of nutrients and the shortage of available water, pumice soils present great challenges to plants.

Flowers, beautiful flowers, grow here, but not in profusion. You will find no carpeted meadows and few streams lined with strips of green. Rather, the plants are scattered about, with a few here and there. Though all is peaceful as you look across the sparse forest, an intense struggle is being waged beneath the surface, a struggle for water and the raw materials from which to build a plant—among the tangled roots, the battle takes place.

With the limited growing season and low productivity, insect life is sparse, too. Lodgepole pine is the dominant tree. The principal shrub is bitterbrush, and the common grass is Idaho fescue. Few other plants can claim to be common here.

It also takes special birds to thrive here. The resources are few. Most are generalists, practicing more than one occupation to make ends meet. Four of the most common species include the Dark-eyed Junco, Yellow-rumped Warbler, Mountain Chickadee, and Western Tanager.

The principal warbler found in these short and open forests is the Yellow-rumped Warbler. If you have an older field guide, you may know this bird as the Audubon's Warbler. The Yellow-rumped Warbler is not your typical warbler. Most are foliage gleaners. Gleaners move quickly through the foliage, searching for insects and other prey at short distances, usually within reach of their temporary perch. It takes a lot of aphids and other small invertebrates to meet the energetic demands of a tiny warm-blooded organism living at high elevations. The Yellow-rumped Warbler is a gleaner, but it employs other tactics as well. Unlike most warblers, it also frequently adopts the behaviors of a flycatcher. Flycatchers scan the air for flying insects from a perch. Upon spotting one, they dart out and pluck the insect from the air and return to perch, often the same perch. At other times it is not unusual to see them hopping along the ground collecting tiny insects. By employing all these methods, Yellow-rumped Warblers succeed in a habitat that might be otherwise too meager to provide an existence.

A single kind of sparrow commonly inhabits the lodgepole pine forests, the Dark-eyed Junco. This is a bit unusual. In most habitats, except for dense forests, two or more species of sparrows coexist. In the grasslands of eastern Oregon, both the Vesper and Brewer's Sparrow serenade visitors in spring. In the oak woodlands in the valleys to the west, it is the Lark and Chipping Sparrow. In the riparian thickets of the high country, it is the White-crowned and Lincoln's Sparrow. However, among the dense lodgepole pines, the Dark-eyed Junco lays sole claim to the seeds and invertebrates found on and near the ground. Adults feed primarily on seeds but take some invertebrates as well, especially when molting. However, a great many seed eating birds, in addition to juncos, turn to a diet rich in protein (insects) when feeding their growing young.

Up among the foliage of the pines, another generalist patrols the forest, the Mountain Chickadee. This resident ekes out a living even in the harshest months of winter by being an opportunist. If a cone offers seeds, it hacks away until the seed yields the prized kernel. A juicy caterpillar is just as greedily consumed. Tiny insect eggs will not be passed up. It searches bark, lichen, foliage, and bud. It searches deep in crevices, inside a curl of bark, among the pine needles and even on the ground. Again, it seems one must employ every trick to earn a living on pumice soils.

Perhaps not as common as the others, the Western Tanager is also a regular inhabitant of the lodgepole pine forest. Like the Yellow-rumped Warbler, it too is both a gleaner and a "flycatcher." However, it forages at a much more sedate pace, scanning both foliage and sky for an insect worthy of pursuit. It will often remain on a single perch for more than a minute as it scans for prey. In contrast, a Yellow-rumped Warbler may visit more than twenty perches in the same amount of time. These differences lead to the capture of different sets of prey.

No discussion of the birds on pumice soils would be complete without mention of two lodgepole pine specialists, Black-backed and American Three-toed Woodpeckers. They are quite similar, and both are not common. The males of both have yellow crowns and both have three toes on each foot. It takes a careful observer to tell them apart. They spend their lives quietly inspecting the trunks of lodgepole pine for burrowing beetle grubs and other insects. Trees recently killed by fire in the lodgepole pine forest attract a host of beetles eager to take advantage of the bounty. These two woodpeckers are quick to take advantage of the abundant source of food. Look for them anywhere you find a stand of recently dead trees.

SURVIVING COLD NIGHTS

The mountain in winter is cold. Biting winds and deep snows make life a challenge for any adventurous enough to brave life above the snow. Even in midsummer the nights turn cold. The thin mountain air retains little heat. Frosts may occur at the rim on any night of the year, and snow flurries are not unheard of on the Fourth of July.

Birds are particularly well adapted to survive in warm environments, including deserts and tropical rainforests. Most operate at a body temperature around 104°F, several degrees higher than that of most mammals. This difference means birds do not suffer thermal stress until a higher ambient temperature. In contrast, this difference in body temperature puts birds at a serious disadvantage in cold environments relative to mammals. Birds must find additional energy on a daily basis compared to mammals of equal mass, all things equal, and high-elevation environments are energy-poor.

Size is one defense against the cold. A large body retains heat because it has less surface area relative to its body volume. The smaller the body, the larger the ratio between surface area and mass and the more difficult it becomes to retain heat. A thick layer of insulation in the form of feathers, fur, or fat helps greatly, but it still can't overcome the disadvantages of being small. You can only put so many feathers on a small bird.

Knowing the relationship between size and surface-to-volume ratios, one might reasonably predict that the smallest birds would be the first to abandon the high country in winter. One might also predict that the birds that breed at higher elevations would be larger, on average, than those lower down.

You would be wrong on both counts. The Golden-crowned Kinglet (0.22 oz) weighs just a bit more than a nickel (0.18 oz.) and is among the smallest birds in the park at any time of year. Yet it is one of a handful of species that winters over. Its winter companions, Red-breasted Nuthatches, Brown Creepers, and Mountain Chickadees, are scarcely larger.

Among breeding birds, one of the smallest sparrows that breeds in Oregon is the Chipping Sparrow. It breeds along the margins of the montane meadows at the rim. The tiny Rufous Hummingbird is common among the penstemons (*Penstemon* spp.) and gilia (*Ipomopsis aggregata*) from May to September. The only slightly larger Golden-crowned Kinglet lives among the forest canopy.

So how do they manage to survive? Instead of fighting the cold, some yield to it! Chickadees, hummingbirds, and some other birds allow their body temperature to drop at night, conserving energy. In general, a drop in body temperature of 18°F reduces metabolic rate (and most chemical reactions) by roughly half. Studies have found that Black-capped Chickadees reduce their body temperature by 11°F–16°F at night, producing considerable savings. Although yet to be studied, it's likely that Mountain Chickadees reduce their body temperature at least as much.

Hummingbirds reduce their body temperature even more, in a process called torpor, maintaining body temperature only a few degrees above ambient temperature, down to 61°F–68°F. Torpor is a kind of short-term hibernation. While in torpor hummingbirds and other animals are largely nonresponsive, and both heart rate and breathing rate are greatly depressed. By allowing body temperature to drop, hummingbirds reduce energy consumption by more than two-thirds, permitting them to survive until sunrise brings new opportunities to find food and fuel their internal fires.

Although a reduction in body temperature or torpor can greatly help individuals conserve energy, it is not an option open to all. Warming back up carries major energetic costs. The cost is proportionately huge for larger animals but relatively small for those who are tiny.

Then there is the time it takes to warm back up. A hummingbird takes about an hour to warm up from as low as 68°F to a normal operating temperature of around 104°F. By comparison, a somewhat larger bird the size of an American Kestrel would take twelve hours to warm up to normal body temperature from 68°F. A significant drop in body temperature works fine for the chickadee but is bad news for larger birds, if they could survive such a drop at all. Larger birds must employ other strategies for coping.

Birds also choose roosting sites that are sheltered. Birds that nest in cavities and crevices tend to roost there as well. The vegetation retained by conifers in winter also helps. These include many of the high-country birds such as chickadees, nuthatches, and woodpeckers. By selecting these sites, the birds are sheltered from both the wind and precipitation, two factors that contribute greatly to the loss of body heat.

Some species, such as Golden-crowned Kinglets, even roost in groups, tightly huddled together or shoulder to shoulder along a limb. Brown Creepers have been discovered to roost in clusters of eight or more individuals. By roosting in close contact, they function as a single larger individual with a much more favorable surface area to volume ratio, thereby conserving energy.

Not many birds have feathered toes, but grouse wear a coat of feathers that keep their feet warm in winter, much like woolen socks. Owls and some other raptors in cold environments also have feathered toes. It takes diverse morphological, physiological, and behavioral strategies to survive in the high country.

Species Accounts

Greater White-Fronted Goose
Anser albifrons

Camping in the park may offer a surprise in late September. On a clear night, with the stars shining bright at 6000 feet, you may hear the approach of geese from out of the northwest. Flight after flight of Greater White-fronted Geese pass over in the darkness as they head for the marshes and fields in the Klamath Basin. Their calls are easily recognized, as they are higher pitched than the calls of the familiar Canada Goose.

Although they rarely, if ever, land on Crater Lake, many use the lake as a navigational checkpoint on their journey to wintering areas. In a relatively few days, thousands pass over the western slopes of Mount Mazama.

As they migrate south, they pause at traditional stopover areas. One of these is Sauvie Island, at the confluence of the Columbia and Willamette Rivers. They rest on the lakes and commute to fields to forage, recovering for the next leg of their journey. As if on cue, most depart within a few days, heading for their next stop. For a great many this includes the Klamath Basin.

The same is repeated in reverse in April as they return north. However, the snows are deep on the rim at this time, and few note their northward migration over the park. This is not their only migratory path in the west, but it is one of the most heavily used.

In 1888, James Merrill witnessed the spring migration while stationed at Fort Klamath, years before the establishment of Crater Lake National Park. Geese by the thousands staged in the fields and marshes at the north end of Upper Klamath Lake, as they had for many years. Flocks ready to complete the next leg of their journey set off on the path that would take them over the western flanks of Mount Mazama on their northward trek. On days when storms pushed up against the slopes of Cascades, flocks were often unable to make the crossing and were forced to return and wait for calmer days.

The short Arctic summer provides little time to raise a family of 4–7. It takes two and a half months to develop from eggs to adult-sized birds ready for the long migration. Greater White-fronted Geese are primarily grazers, but they are equally content gleaning leftover grain from harvested fields.

Description: A relatively small goose (28") with a pink bill, orange feet, and black markings on the belly of the adults. The white tail has a broad

Greater White-fronted Geese

Greater White-fronted Goose

black band, and its name comes from a narrow ring of white feathers surrounding the bill.

Distribution: White-fronted Geese occur broadly in North America, breeding on river deltas and tundra of Alaska and Canada. In winter they migrate to the southern United States and northern Mexico. Some that breed in eastern Siberia cross over into North America and migrate down the Pacific Coast. At Crater Lake National Park they are an abundant migrant over the park on their spring and fall migrations.

Common Merganser
Mergus merganser

A small flock of ducks swims near the shoreline of Crater Lake. Silently they dive in the clear water seeking small fish and crayfish. Their bodies are silvered by the film of air clinging to their bodies as they search among the rocks at the bottom of the shallows. A short while later they bob to the surface, sending ripples across the calm waters. One holds a fish in its bill and tosses it down. Another finds a small crayfish. This is repeated many times before all are sated. Eventually, they retreat to a small rocky beach to rest and warm themselves in the cool mountain sun.

Common Mergansers are a common sight on Crater Lake today, but 150 years ago, they would have visited the lake only rarely. There would have been little reason to stay. Prior to the introduction of rainbow trout, kokanee, and crayfish, there would have been little suitable food.

Common Mergansers are larger than most ducks and float low in the water. They are built for speed under water more than for buoyancy. A denser body makes it easier to remain submerged while in pursuit of agile prey. Like all mergansers, they have a thin bill with short, tooth-like spikes along the edges. The projections are not bone or enamel but keratin, like the covering of the bill or fingernails. The "teeth" help them hold on to slippery prey.

Their simple nest, composed largely of feathers, is placed in a tree cavity, among the rocks of a talus slope, or deep within dense vegetation. The 9–12 eggs hatch in 32 days, and the young are ready to fly at 9–10 weeks of age. They molt during the summer and are flightless for a few weeks. During this time the males are in eclipse plumage and look much like the females. Males soon undergo a second molt in the fall, this time to regain their bright breeding plumage. Family groups often remain together throughout the winter.

Many other ducks briefly visit Crater Lake including Mallards, Northern Shovelers, Lesser Scaup, and Ruddy Ducks, but none remain long. Most are migrants, using the lake as a place to rest up before the next segment of their journey.

Description: A large duck (25"). The male merganser has a body that is largely white. The head is dark green with a long, thin, pink bill. The female has a gray body, light belly, and a reddish-brown head with a shaggy crest. In flight both show white wing patches.

Common Merganser, male

Common Merganser, females

Distribution: A common species throughout North America along streams, rivers, and lakes. Common Mergansers also occur in Europe and Asia, where it is called a Goosander. In winter the northern populations retreat southward to the southern United States. At Crater Lake National Park, it occurs in small numbers along the shores of Crater Lake from spring to fall and sometimes breeds.

Sooty Grouse
Dendragapus fuliginosus

Perhaps the most startling experience in the park is not a chance encounter with a bear or other predator but something much less threatening. A Sooty Grouse sitting tight in a meadow may lose its nerve and erupt from nearly underfoot. Flapping wildly at first, it glides off for a safe retreat.

When not flushed, they are remarkably tame and are most often seen standing still along the roadside quite unimpressed with passing cars. In older field guides, the name for this bird is Blue Grouse. In 2006 it was recognized that the Blue Grouse actually encompassed two species, the Sooty Grouse of the Cascades and Sierras and the Dusky Grouse of the Rocky Mountains.

When courting, the male Sooty Grouse typically finds a large horizontal limb high in a tree and "booms." The deep, repetitive hooting sounds much like a large owl and has fooled many people. The caller is difficult to locate even when very close. As they display, they inflate two yellow neck pouches.

Each year they undertake an annual altitudinal migration. They amble downhill in the spring to breed and work their way back up into the high country for winter. Seemingly backward, perhaps, but in winter they feed on the buds of evergreens while safely concealed and sheltered from bitter winds under the protective blanket of snow.

Another grouse, the Ruffed Grouse, also occurs in the park. It is browner, with a small crest and a black band near the end of the reddish-brown or gray tail. It occurs most often along the streams at lower elevations.

Sooty Grouse feed on a wide variety of food gleaned from the ground or low vegetation, including both invertebrates and plants (buds and fruit). The nest is a simple depression in thick vegetation lined with feathers and a bit of grass. It lays 6–7 eggs that hatch after a 26-day incubation. The precocial young leave the nest almost immediately after hatching and follow the female. As with most grouse and quail, the flight feathers develop very rapidly and the young, barely more than a ball of fluff, can fly at the age of just over a week—a useful skill, given the number of terrestrial predators.

Description: Large birds (20"), about the size of a chicken, grayish in color with a broad, gray band at the end of a black tail. The males have

Sooty Grouse, female

Sooty Grouse, male

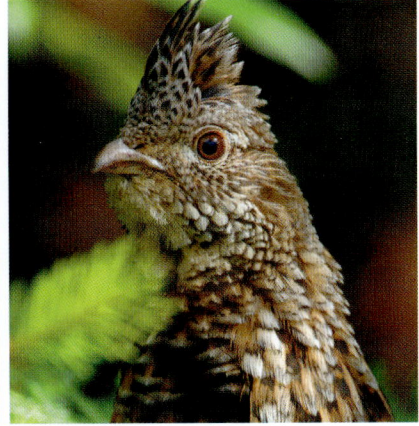

Ruffed Grouse

inflatable throat pouches. The pouches are highlighted in white by the bases of the surrounding feathers when inflated. The female is browner and more mottled than the male.

Distribution: Sooty Grouse occur in and near conifer forests in the Cascades and Sierra Nevada. In Crater Lake National Park they are widespread, extending their range from the lower-elevation forests into the mountain meadows. They are less common among ponderosa pines in the drier portions of the park to the east.

Common Nighthawk
Chordeiles minor

Late in the afternoon, Common Nighthawks rouse from their day roosts on tree limbs, fence posts, and bare gravel soils. As the sun begins to settle in the west, they take flight on long wings, heading out to greet the insects rising from the forests and meadows. The white bars in the wings show prominently even in the fading light.

Their large mouth is bordered by bristles that make it even easier to capture elusive flying insects. The mouth is so large that people once thought they suckled goats, giving the name goatsuckers to the family of birds that includes both nighthawks and Whip-poor-wills. Instead, nighthawks were simply drawn to the insects flying around the livestock.

Nighthawks are the last spring migrant to arrive in Oregon, usually making their appearance around Memorial Day. They are most often observed in the hour before complete darkness over the slopes of Mount Mazama, but they can be heard during the night giving a short harsh call note as they fly. Besides the nasal call, nighthawks make another sound, this one with their wings. While flying high, they dive. As they pull out of the dive, they hold their wings rigid. The wind rushing over the tips of their wings causes them to vibrate, making a sound much like a truck passing in the distance. They reportedly make this sound during court-ship and in defense of the nest.

Nighthawks feed exclusively on flying insects captured while cours-ing above forests and fields. They build no nest but lay two cryptically colored eggs in a shallow depression on a sandy or gravelly area, often on a ridge. Incubation lasts about 18 days and the young fledge at about 17–18 days. Nighthawks frequently assemble into large flocks in August in preparation for the southward migration.

A close relative is occasionally detected in the park, the Common Poorwill. The bird is named for its call and hunts flying insects while perched on the ground.

Description: Common Nighthawks (9.5") are the size of a dove. The back is mottled gray-brown and the belly is finely barred. The long pointed wings are marked with a distinctive white patch on the prima-ries. The male has a small white throat and small white marks in the tail, marks that are lacking in the female.

Common Nighthawk

Common Nighthawk

Distribution: Breeds throughout North America from northern Canada to Mexico and winters in northern South America. At Crater Lake National Park they are regular visitors throughout the summer. A few nest on the bare pumice soils at the lower elevations and are most easily observed in the drier portions of the park.

Rufous Hummingbird
Selasphorus rufus

The mountain meadows are a favored seasonal stopover point for Rufous Hummingbirds. For those breeding at lower elevations, once duties are complete, they follow the flowers of spring up into the mountains, ending at places like the rim of Crater Lake. Here they tenaciously defend briefly held feeding territories against other hummingbirds. Some breed in the park, but many more visit. They favor red flowers including columbine, Indian paintbrush, and skyrocket gilia. Hummingbird-pollinated flowers also tend to be tubular, and contain abundant nectar that usually has a lower sugar concentration than insect-pollinated flowers. To complete their meal, they must visit many flowers. In this way plants ensure their pollen is broadly distributed. Hummingbirds supplement their diet with small flying insects that provide needed protein. Many insects are unable to see red, a color clearly seen by hummingbirds.

For brightly colored males, the breeding season is over very early, for they contribute little to the reproductive effort. Males neither incubate the eggs nor feed the young. Once the young have fledged, the females and young join the males in the high country. After a time, and with a sufficient store of fat, they make the leap south, where they feed on the flowers along the way and, finally, winter in western Mexico. Their voice is unimpressive, but the wings of the male create a distinctive metallic whine when it flies.

When courting, hummingbirds perform spectacular aerial displays unique to each species. The Rufous Hummingbird starts high in the air and dives steeply, tracing a J-shape, with the bottom of the "J" just inches above the perched female.

The nest is constructed of spider silk and plant fibers and decorated with moss and lichen. Invariably two eggs are laid, and the incubation period is 15–17 days. The young spend 3 weeks in the nest before fledging.

Description: The male (3.75") is orange above and below with an iridescent red throat. The female and young are green above and white below with a rufous wash on the sides and in the tail.

Distribution: Rufous Hummingbirds breed from southeast Alaska through the Rockies and coastal states to northern California. Most winter in western Mexico. In the park they are common and widespread

Rufous Hummingbird, male

Rufous Hummingbird, female

in the summer wherever flowers are blooming. The adult males depart earlier in the summer than the females and young.

Spotted Sandpiper

Actitis macularius

A small brown bird patrols the shore of the lake. If flushed, it will most likely give a loud double flute-like note of protest as it flies off with quick, shallow wing beats on stiff wings. Staying close to the water's surface, it swings out over the lake before returning to land a short way off. Unperturbed, it continues its relentless search for food. Not many sandpipers are at home along the shores of high mountain lakes or on the gravel bars of rivers locally, but the Spotted Sandpiper is an exception. Unlike most of the smaller shorebirds, which join flocks during migration and on wintering beaches, it feeds alone at all times of the year.

It teeters as it gleans small invertebrates from the water's edge. Tail-bobbing helps an individual communicate with its young and others that may be nearby in noisy environments such as along rushing streams. In this respect it is like the Dipper, another bird that finds visual cues to be more effective than calls. Unlike many sandpipers, it seldom wades in the water.

The Spotted Sandpiper has what seems an unusual breeding system. The parental roles are "reversed." Instead of males courting females, as in a great many birds, the larger female courts the male. After courtship, and once the 4-egg clutch is complete, the female flies off in search of another mate, leaving the male to incubate the eggs for 21 days and care for the young for about 4 weeks. The nest is a simple depression among short vegetation near the shoreline. Scientists refer to this mating system as "polyandry" (one female and several males) or, more appropriately, "serial monogamy," reflecting the series of brief pair bonds.

This arrangement is not unusual among shorebirds. Phalaropes also exhibit reversed parental roles. Not only are the females larger than the males but they are also more brightly colored. Bright colors and sexual dimorphism are uncommon among shorebirds.

The Spotted Sandpiper is the only shorebird likely to be encountered in Crater Lake National Park. The marshes in the Klamath Basin, in contrast, harbor several breeding species and thousands of migrants.

Description: A small bird (7.5") with a brown back and an orange bill. The white underparts are boldly spotted during the breeding season but a uniform white in winter. Watch for the white stripe that runs the length of the wing when it flies.

Spotted Sandpiper, breeding

Spotted Sandpiper, nonbreeding

Distribution: Widely distributed across North America. In winter most Spotted Sandpipers migrate to the southern United States or Central America. At Crater Lake National Park they arrive on the shores of the lake and along Annie Creek in May and remain until September.

California Gull
Larus californicus

Out on the lake, a small flock of gulls swims quietly. A few more individuals fly lazily about, apparently looking for anything edible in the waters. The pale gray backs of these birds look nearly white to visitors viewing the lake from the rim. Their long narrow wings allow them to fly easily while expending little energy.

More than twelve species of gulls can be found in Oregon, but only four breed. Of these only one regularly visits the lake, the California Gull. It is a relatively small gull, smaller than the Western Gull that breeds and winters along the Oregon coast. As California Gulls travel between their wintering areas along the coast and their breeding areas in marshes and along lakes in the interior of the continent, small flocks often pause on the lake to rest and feed a bit.

They are opportunists and feed on a variety of invertebrates, small fish, and even carrion. At other times they are content gleaning seeds from fields.

It takes California Gulls four years to attain full adult plumage and breed for the first time. Since there always seem to be a few birds on the lake throughout the summer, many of those lingering appear to be subadult birds.

The nearest colony of breeding California Gulls is in the marshes of Upper Klamath Lake. They nest colonially on the ground on small predator-free islands or in dense marsh vegetation. Despite breeding colonially, they are intensely territorial, defending a relatively small area about the nest. Inattentive parents may lose both eggs and small young to neighboring birds. They are monogamous and lay 2–3 cryptically colored eggs in a modest nest constructed of vegetation. The incubation period is about 24–27 days, and the young fledge in about 7 weeks.

Description: Adult gulls (21") have a white head and body with a gray back and wings. The primaries are tipped in black, each with a small white dot at the tip. The bill is pale yellow, and the legs range in color from pale green to yellow. Unlike most other gulls, California Gulls have both a red and black spot on the bill. Immature birds are browner and are challenging to distinguish from other gulls. Male and female are similar.

Distribution: The California Gull breeds in the Intermountain West and in the prairie states and provinces. In winter they tend to migrate to the

California Gull

California Gull

coast, though some remain on open inland water. They visit Crater Lake throughout the warmer months but do not nest in Crater Lake National Park.

Sharp-shinned Hawk, Cooper's Hawk, American Goshawk

Accipiter striatus, Astur cooperii, Astur atricapillus

The three forest hawks, commonly known as accipiters, are primarily bird hunters. Recently, the Cooper's Hawk and American Goshawk were removed from the genus Accipiter and placed in the genus Astur.

Seldom leaving the cover of the forest, accipiters dash into an area hoping to surprise a bird at close range. Failing at this, they perch silently, waiting for a concealed bird to move. Once a bird betrays its location, the hawk strikes quickly, often in a chase that is a test of agility of both predator and prey in dense habitat. Their relatively short wings and long tail allow for quick acceleration and great maneuverability. Accipiters also have excellent hearing, and hunt by sound as well as sight.

The Sharp-shinned Hawk is the smallest and most common. The Cooper's Hawk is larger but similar in appearance to the Sharp-shinned Hawk. The American Goshawk is the largest. Both the Cooper's Hawk and American Goshawk tend to breed in the warmer and drier portions of the park, while Sharp-shinned Hawks favor the cooler areas in the forest.

Sharp-shinned Hawks feed almost entirely on small birds; the larger accipiters eat mammals as well. Often the first clue that an accipiter is near is the alarm call given by chipmunks and golden-mantled ground squirrels.

Males are smaller than females in all three species. Male Sharp-shinned Hawks weigh just half as much as the females. One possible explanation is that males are more agile by virtue of their smaller size, and this makes them more efficient hunters, which is important since they provide most of the food for the young. Other hawks are noted for their skill in soaring, but forest hawks do so only occasionally.

Their nest is a stick nest built on a horizontal limb, usually against the trunk, and lined with flakes of bark. The 3–5 eggs are incubated for 4 weeks and the young fledge after 30–34 days. Accipiters attain adult plumage at the beginning of their second year and breed the following year.

Description: The adult Sharp-shinned Hawk (11") is a slender bird with long legs and short wings. Both male and female are slate gray above and finely barred brick red below. The long tail is banded black and gray with a narrow white tip. The eye is bright orange or red. Cooper's Hawks (16") are almost identical in color and shape but larger. American Goshawks

Sharp-shinned Hawk, adult

Cooper's Hawk, adult

American Goshawk, adult

(21") are larger still, but the adult is silver-gray below. First-year birds of all three are brown above and streaked brown below, and the eye is a pale yellow.

Distribution: The three species occur from Alaska and Canada south into Mexico. The easiest time of year to observe them at Crater Lake is during fall migration in late August and September. At this time of year, they typically leave the cover of the forest and soar and glide along the ridgelines as they pass south.

Bald Eagle
Haliaeetus leucocephalus

High in a conifer above the lake, an adult Bald Eagle perches on a large limb. The white head stands out against the dark trees and talus hillside behind. From its perch it scans the waters for fish near the surface. Once the target is spotted, the eagle takes flight on wings measuring 7 feet across. It glides silently to the surface of the lake and neatly plucks an unsuspecting fish from the water.

Individual birds often visit the lake, but only in recent years have they have begun to breed. Originally, there were no fish in Crater Lake. However, between 1888 and 1941, salmon and trout were introduced with the hope of providing for recreational fishing. Today kokanee and rainbow trout provide a food source for the Bald Eagle. Compared to other areas such as Upper Klamath Lake, there is little other prey available for Bald Eagles.

The recovery of the Bald Eagle from its historic population lows in the 1960s is a remarkable story. Pesticides, specifically DDT and its metabolites, were taken up by a variety of animals, especially aquatic organisms, and further concentrated with each step up the food chain. Bald Eagles, sitting atop the food chain, received the highest doses. DDE, the metabolite of DDT, interferes with the metabolism of calcium, and the eggs of affected birds had thin shells that easily broke or allowed the eggs to dehydrate during incubation. Since restrictions on the use of DDT, Bald Eagles have recovered, and are once again a familiar sight. The Klamath Basin, just south of Crater Lake National Park, is famous for its large wintering population of Bald Eagles. More than 100 eagles can be observed in a day around the marshes of the national wildlife refuges. Several pairs nest along the shore of Upper Klamath Lake.

Bald Eagles feed largely on fish, water birds, and carrion. Coots are a favored prey in winter. Eagles construct a bulky nest of sticks, most often in a tree, but sometimes also on cliffs or even on the ground. They frequently reuse the same nest, adding new sticks each year. One to 3 eggs are incubated for 35 days. Young fledge in 6–14 weeks.

Description. Adults (31") have a dark brown, almost black, body with a white head and tail. The bill and feet are yellow. First-year birds are all dark including the bill. Second-year birds are largely dark on the head and back but have a mottled white chest, belly, and underwings. Full adult

Bald Eagle, adult

Bald Eagle, immature

plumage is acquired by the fourth year. Young birds can be easily confused with the Golden Eagle, which also occurs on occasion in the park. Ospreys, with their whitish head, are sometimes mistaken for adult Bald Eagles.

Distribution: Found from northern Alaska and Canada to northern Mexico. They are partially migratory. Within Crater Lake National Park, a single pair breeds along the shores of the lake but not every year.

Red-tailed Hawk
Buteo jamaicensis

Emerging from the trees at the edge of the Pumice Desert, a large hawk glides fast and low out over the mountain meadow. Just before striking, the hawk pulls up sharply, breaking off the attack. It flaps slowly back to its perch to continue its search for a meal. The targeted western pocket gopher detected the attacking hawk just in time and retreated quickly from the unfinished mound of dirt. It comes as a surprise to many that pocket gophers are a major food of Red-tailed Hawks. Unlike some of their relatives, Red-tailed Hawks are "sit-and-wait" predators, often seen sitting high on an exposed perch waiting patiently for some rodent or snake or other small animal to venture just a bit too far from cover. They soar most often when patrolling their territory, monitoring their neighbor's activities or those of strangers. It is also important for them to watch for Golden Eagles, which will take an unwary hawk.

In late summer numerous hawks scour the meadows for prey. At lower elevations ground squirrels have already retreated to dens to sleep away the remainder of the summer, fall, and winter, a sleep that may last eight months. As prey becomes scarce at the lower elevations, many hawks head upslope, where it is still spring in the mountain meadows and prey are more active.

Many of these hawks are juveniles and do not yet wear the orange tail of the adults. Before the snow comes all will have retreated to places like the Klamath Basin and points farther south, where hunting is easier and the weather more hospitable.

Red-tailed Hawks construct a large stick nest in a tree or on a cliff ledge, where they lay 1–4 eggs, 2–3 being most common. The period of incubation is 35 days, and the young fledge in about 6 weeks. After fledging they are fed in diminishing amounts as the adults encourage them to sharpen their foraging skills. Many never fully master the skills necessary for survival, and more than half fail to survive their first year of independence.

Description: A large hawk (19"), brown on the back and usually light below, with a belly band that varies in darkness among individuals. The tail of adults is orange and is obtained in the second year of life. Dark-phase individuals, with entirely dark underparts, are less common. Immatures have a brown tail banded in black.

Red-tailed Hawk, adult

Red-tailed Hawk, adult

Distribution: Red-tailed Hawks occur throughout North America in a diversity of habitats from northern Canada and Alaska to Central America and the Caribbean. Birds in colder climates, including much of Oregon east of the Cascades, migrate to southerly areas. During September and October, migrant birds can be frequently seen heading south along the ridges and other high points.

Great Horned Owl
Bubo virginianus

As the last vestiges of light fade from the sky, a deep hooting is heard from the trees on the far side of a meadow. The call starts with two or three short notes and ends with three drawn-out notes. It is answered by its mate on a slightly different pitch from some distance away. The call of the male is typically deeper.

Great Horned Owls patrol the edges of the forest and throughout open woodlands, seeking almost anything that moves and is small enough to capture. In addition to their typical fare of small mammals, birds, and snakes, they have been known to eat skunks, porcupines, lizards, scorpions, ants, and even other owls. The familiar "owl-like" face helps collect the faint sounds from potential prey. Species of owls that hunt by day as well as by night have a much less pronounced facial disk.

It is commonly thought that the silent flight of owls is due to the need to silently approach prey without alerting them. This may be partially true, but more importantly, it allows the owl to monitor the quiet sounds an animal makes during an attack. In the dark of night, prey may be located entirely by sound. These sounds would be much more difficult to detect if the air created noise as it rushed over the wings of the flying owl.

Owls build no nest of their own but use natural cavities and depressions in cliffs and broken treetops. They frequently use the old nests of other birds, such as those of Red-tailed Hawks and Common Ravens. The 2–3 eggs are incubated for about 35 days, and the young fledge at 6 weeks of age, full-sized and fully feathered, though down may still cling to their feathers.

The Great Horned Owl is just one of several owls that occur in the park. They range in size from the tiny Northern Pygmy-Owl, the size of a robin, to the large Great Gray Owl. Others include Northern Saw-whet Owl, Flammulated Owl, Western Screech-Owl, Long-eared Owl, Barred Owl, and Spotted Owl.

Description: The Great Horned Owl is a large owl (22") about the size of a large hawk with a large facial disk and ear-like tufts of feathers. Plumage is heavily marked, including finely barred underparts. Ear-like tufts of feathers or "horns" aid in concealment from jays and other birds that would harass them during the day. They have nothing to do with hearing. The female is larger than the male.

Great Horned Owl, adult

Great Horned Owl, juvenile

Distribution: Great Horned Owls occur from the edge of the tundra in Canada and Alaska to southern Central America. They are found in almost every habitat from desert to tropical rainforest and avoid only the deepest forests. In Crater Lake National Park, they are most often detected at timberline and in the drier more open habitats near the southern boundary of the park.

Lewis's Woodpecker
Melanerpes lewis

The Lewis's Woodpecker is a different kind of woodpecker. They are not as adept at drilling into sound wood to expose beetle grubs as are many other woodpeckers. Instead, they have a more varied diet. They commonly sally out to pluck insects from the air like a flycatcher. Fruits and berries are prized when available. In winter, they favor oaks. Like the Acorn Woodpecker, they harvest and store acorns, although they do not construct the impressive granaries of their close relatives.

Meriwether Lewis wrote about the black woodpecker on his expedition, remarking on its crow-like appearance. In flight it behaves much like a crow, with slow wing beats. Most woodpeckers have an undulating flight, wherein they flap for a few quick beats and rise, then fold their wings and coast.

Lewis's Woodpeckers are one of the few woodpeckers in the west that are strongly migratory, and their movements are often noteworthy, with 500 or more passing a given point on a single day. On a clear September day, a fortunate observer may encounter a steady parade of them working their way one or two at a time over the crest of the Cascades, heading for the oak-filled valleys of southwestern Oregon and points south where they spend the winter.

Lewis's Woodpeckers are seldom common anywhere in Oregon during the breeding season, and their numbers have declined over the last several decades. The reasons for their decline are poorly understood.

The nest is excavated in the trunk of a tree. Like other cavity-nesting birds, clutches tend to be relatively large. The 5–7 white eggs are incubated for 12–16 days, largely by the female. Both parents feed the young.

Description: The Lewis's Woodpecker (11") is a very dark woodpecker, appearing black in all but the best of lighting. Up close they reveal beautiful colors. The back has a faint iridescent green sheen. The face is brick red and the belly is pink. The gray collar is often the only clear feature seen in poor light.

Distribution: Occurs in a patchy breeding distribution throughout the intermountain region of western North America, favoring riparian forests in open country extending from southern British Columbia to the southern Rocky Mountains. While a few may occasionally breed in the

Lewis's Woodpecker

Lewis's Woodpecker

southeastern corner of the park, they are most frequently seen in fall migration.

Red-breasted Sapsucker and Williamson's Sapsucker
Sphyrapicus ruber and S. thyroideus

Drrrrrrrrrum-drum-drum. The distinctive cadence of drumming heralds the presence of a sapsucker somewhere in the forest. Other than drumming they are quiet birds, calling rarely, making them difficult to observe. Three species of these unique woodpeckers may be found in the park. The most common and most striking is the Red-breasted Sapsucker, with its red hood and breast. The closely related Red-naped Sapsucker is a rare visitor. The third species, the Williamson's Sapsucker, is most often encountered east of the crest of the Cascades and among the ponderosa pine but can be found in other forest types as well. Williamson's Sapsuckers are unique among the woodpeckers of our region. Where males and females of most woodpeckers are quite similar, male and female Williamson's Sapsuckers bear little resemblance to each other.

As the name sapsucker suggests, all feed on sap harvested from a series of small, shallow holes drilled into the bark of a tree. The sap wells are often arranged in neat horizontal rows around the trunk. They cause little damage to the tree and provide a dependable food supply. Whereas most woodpeckers have an extremely long tongue with a hard and sharpened tip for harpooning insects burrowing in trees, the tongue of the sapsucker is much shorter and brushy-tipped, better for lapping up sap. Sap is often used by trees to repel beetles attempting to enter the tree and contains chemicals that function as insecticides. Apparently, this is not an impediment for sapsuckers.

Other birds have learned to drink from these sap wells, including Ruby-crowned Kinglets, hummingbirds, and Yellow-rumped Warblers Many insects also take advantage of the resource, including butterflies, moths, bees, and wasps. In addition to sap, sapsuckers also eat insects and fruit when available.

Their nest is a cavity, usually excavated in a tree with little more than a few wood chips for a nest. The female lays 4–6 white eggs that are incubated for 12–14 days, and the young fledge in about 31 days.

Description: Male and female Red-breasted Sapsuckers (9") are similar. The head and breast are carmine red, and the back is marked with white. Large white patches in the wings are obvious when the bird flies. Male Williamson's Sapsuckers (9") are black with a red chin and white rump

Red-breasted Sapsucker

Williamson's Sapsucker, male

and wing patches. The female has a brownish head and a barred back. All have a yellow belly.

Distribution: Both species occur from western Canada to northern Mexico. Red-breasted Sapsuckers are common among firs throughout the park. Williamson's Sapsuckers overlap with the Red-breasted Sapsucker but are more often found in the eastern portions of the park. Most sapsuckers depart in winter and arrive in April.

American Three-toed Woodpecker and Black-backed Woodpecker

Picoides dorsalis and P. arcticus

A severely burned forest, one that bears little more than blackened poles in an ashy landscape, gives the feeling that something precious has been lost. Yet nature doesn't view the event as a tragedy. It is a part of the natural cycle of forests in this region, shaped by fires for many thousands of years. It is a time of rebirth. Seeds are germinating that quickly bring new green to the hillsides. A walk among the ashes the spring following a stand-replacing fire will reveal abundant conifer seedlings. The shell of a seed may cling briefly to a small cluster of needles perched on a spindly stem emerging from the soil. This is the forest to be. Other locations that are less intensely burned may find a lupine growing strong or some other plant growing from the roots protected under the surface. And you might hear soft drilling. A pair of Black-backed Woodpeckers also finds life inside the blackened trunks.

Even as the ashes cooled the previous year, both metallic and long-horned wood-boring beetles were attracted by the chemicals released by the burning trees. Black-backed and Three-toed Woodpeckers are quick to appear. For the first couple of years after the fire, there will be bounty. Grubs of these beetles will be abundant in galleries beneath the bark and tunnels within the wood. How these woodpeckers find and congregate in recent burns is something of a mystery. Most birds are not known for their powers of smell, but it's interesting to consider that these woodpeckers may use the same chemical cues released by damaged trees as the beetles to find recently burned areas. When not chasing fires, both live at low densities in lodgepole pine forests.

The two woodpeckers are closely related. Both have three toes on each foot, whereas most woodpeckers have four, and their overall black color makes them all but invisible on the fire-blackened trunks. Like most woodpeckers, they drill a cavity in a tree, often dead, for a nest. The 3–5 white eggs are incubated for 11–14 days. Both parents tend the young for the 22–26 days before they fledge.

Description. Both species (9") are glossy black above with white under parts. Both have barring on the flanks and narrow white lines on the face. The males have a small yellow patch on the top of the head. The two species differ in that the American Three-toed Woodpecker has at least

American Three-toed Woodpecker

Black-backed Woodpecker

some white on the back. The American Three-toed Woodpeckers of the southern Oregon Cascades have very little white on the back compared with those in other areas.

Distribution: Both species occur broadly across the boreal forests. The Black-backed Woodpecker occurs as far south as the Sierra Nevada of California and southern Idaho in the Rocky Mountains. The American Three-toed Woodpecker occurs as far south as the Crater Lake area in the Oregon Cascades and the southern Rocky Mountains in Arizona and New Mexico.

Hairy Woodpecker
Dryobates villosus

The grubs of wood-boring insects are a reliable food resource: they have few defenses, they are slow to mature, and they can be found year-round even in the middle of winter. The only challenge is that they are in tunnels under thick bark or deep in the wood, usually in dead trees.

It takes a special predator to access this resource. First, the predator must expose the gallery or tunnel and then, having opened it, must extract the grub residing some distance down the tunnel. Woodpeckers are well-designed for the task. They have a powerful beak for opening the tunnels, as well as strong feet, a stout tail that acts as a prop, and a cushioned brain that protects the bird while hammering on a trunk. Once the tunnel is opened, the woodpecker extends an extraordinarily long tongue down the channel. The tip of the tongue is hardened, with barbs like a fishhook used to stab the grub and retrieve it. The tongue can be extended far into the tunnel because it is not anchored under the chin, as it is in most birds. A typical tongue inserted under the chin can be extended only a short distance. Remarkably, the tongue of a woodpecker, when retracted, continues around behind the head, up over the skull, and inserts in the right nostril!

Other animals around the world attempt to exploit the same wood-shielded resource, but none are as well-adapted as woodpeckers. In the Galapagos Islands, the Woodpecker Finch has a stout bill for opening galleries and uses a twig or cactus spine to pry out the grubs. The New Caledonian Crow fashions tools from leaves to function as a woodpecker tongue. In Madagascar a lemur called the aye-aye fills the same niche. Their rodent-like incisors are used to bite into the wood to open the tunnels. It then uses its extremely long and slender middle finger to probe for and remove grubs.

The Hairy Woodpecker is the most common woodpecker in western forests. It is at home in almost any forest type in Oregon including Douglas-fir, white fir, mountain hemlock, ponderosa pine, lodgepole pine, and even riparian woodland and oak savanna when not breeding. Their nest is chiseled into a tree and holds 3–0 white eggs. Incubation lasts 11–12 days, and both parents feed the young before they fledge at 28–30 days.

Description: Male and female (9.25") are black above with a white back, black-and-white face pattern and spots on the wing. They are white

Hairy Woodpecker, male

Hairy Woodpecker, female

below. The male has a small red patch on the back of the head. They are similar to the Downy Woodpecker, which rarely appears in the park. Downy Woodpeckers are smaller and have a proportionately shorter bill. **Distribution:** Hairy Woodpeckers are widespread in forested habitats throughout North America and Mexico. In Oregon and Crater Lake National Park they are a widespread but uncommon resident.

White-headed Woodpecker
Dryobates arbolarvatus

A quiet rain of debris filters down from high in a ponderosa pine. The falling wood chips caught in the sunlight filtering through the tree may be the only sign that a White-headed Woodpecker is in the vicinity. Sound offers little help in finding the source of the disturbance. This bird seldom calls, and even when it does, the simple call is very soft. Patience and a careful search among the shadows may eventually reveal a jet-black woodpecker with a striking white head. The White-headed Woodpecker looks more like a toy than a real bird.

Male and female woodpeckers tend to forage in different ways. In Downy Woodpeckers, females tend to search the smaller outer branches of a tree for insects while the male remains on the trunk and larger branches. The differences in foraging behavior are greater still in the White-headed Woodpecker. Males frequently hang from a branch and dismantle ponderosa cones, working diligently for a dinner of seeds. Females tend to forage in a more traditional fashion, probing and drilling the trunks and branches of pines for beetle grubs and other insects beneath the bark.

The preference of White-headed Woodpeckers for mature and old-growth ponderosa pines has contributed to a marked population decline. Timber harvest has reduced the abundance of older trees, and fire suppression has contributed to an invasion of other tree species such as white fir, making the habitat less suitable.

For a nest, White-headed Woodpeckers usually drill a hole in a dead tree or stump, often quite close to the ground. They incubate a clutch of 4–5 white eggs for 14 days, and the young fledge in about 26 days.

Description: White-headed Woodpeckers (9") are uniform black with a white head. The male has a small red mark on the back of the head. They have a distinctive small white patch at the base of the primaries that is obvious when it flies. Only the Acorn Woodpecker among our local woodpeckers has a similar mark. The white patch in the wings of sapsuckers is much closer to the body

Distribution: White-headed Woodpeckers are resident in ponderosa pines from southern British Columbia, south through the Cascades and Blue Mountains to the Sierra Nevada. At higher elevations they occur

White-headed Woodpecker, male

White-headed Woodpecker, female

at low densities among white fir. At Crater Lake National Park they are most often seen in the pines near the southern entrance.

Northern Flicker
Colaptes auratus

A solitary brown bird a bit larger than a robin flushes from the ground at the edge of a meadow and flies off into the forest. The white rump shows brightly, but the wary bird noticed the hikers at a considerable distance and offered only a poor look. The Northern Flicker is a brightly colored bird, but it is difficult to approach if you want to appreciate the stunning salmon-colored linings of the wing and tail in the western form. More often hikers find an occasional molted feather.

The Northern Flicker is a woodpecker with some rather odd behaviors. It is one of the very few woodpeckers that feeds primarily on the ground. They probe the ground much like a sandpiper probes the mud on a mudflat. Their brown back helps conceal them as they feed. Flickers favor ants as prey. Ants are chemically challenging food, containing formic acid. Few animals can tolerate a steady diet of ants, and those that can form a rather eclectic group including, among others, anteaters, horned lizards, and echidnas. So, is the beak of the flicker wasted? Not at all. In every other way it is a typical woodpecker. It drills a standard cavity in a tree for its nest and hammers on trees to announce its presence and attract mates. The more resonant the substrate for hammering, the better. Unfortunately for some unlucky homeowners, if gutters and metal flashing are discovered by a male, the result is a repeated jarring announcement from the territory holder, often beginning before daybreak.

In addition to ants, it also feeds on fruit and other insects. A pair typically rears 5–9 young. The incubation period is 11 days and the young fledge 24–27 days after hatching.

Description: Northern Flickers (12") have a brown back, finely barred in black, and a white rump. There is a black crescent on their chest, and the pinkish brown belly is heavily spotted. The color pattern of the head and underwings vary among populations. The western "Red-shafted" Flicker of western North America has salmon-colored linings to the wing and tail.

Distribution: Northern Flickers are found across North America. They prefer open woodlands and the edges of forests rather than dense stands. Populations in colder regions are migratory. In Crater Lake National Park they are uncommon but widespread summer residents and rare

Northern Flicker, male

Northern Flicker, female

winter residents at the lowest elevations wherever meadows and open woodlands occur.

Pileated Woodpecker
Dryocopus pileatus

The surprisingly loud staccato call ringing through the forest is often the first clue that a pair of crow-sized Pileated Woodpeckers is about. The second clue may be the rectangular holes, large and small, drilled into decaying snags. The reason for this geometric preference is unclear. These birds can be quite tame, especially if they are intently feeding on a fallen log. You can sometimes approach quite closely.

Most woodpeckers are about the size of a robin. The Downy Woodpecker is a bit smaller, the Northern Flicker a bit larger. Then there is the Pileated Woodpecker. It is the largest woodpecker in the forests of Crater Lake National Park by far, and in most of North America as well.

The Pileated Woodpecker is relatively common throughout its range. Its continued success is due, in part, to its generalized habitat requirements, including most forest types, even oaks. Its larger cousin, the Ivory-billed Woodpecker, almost certainly extinct, was a specialist on old-growth riparian forests that flooded each year in the Mississippi River drainage and other southeastern rivers, a habitat that has largely vanished.

Pileated Woodpeckers feed on beetle grubs and other insects found beneath bark and burrowing in wood, but they have a particular preference for ants, especially large carpenter ants. Ants are not a preferred food for many species because of the irritating chemicals they contain, as well as their swarming defense when a colony is exposed. These strategies don't seem to slow down the Pileated Woodpecker.

Carpenter ants are especially common in white fir forests, in part because white firs are susceptible to heart rot. The softened wood is easily colonized by ants. Carpenter ants are predators and do not feed on the wood as do termites, but they do burrow in wood as a place to live.

The 3–5 white eggs are laid in a cavity chiseled in a tree and are incubated for 16–18 days. Both parents care for the young, which fledge in about 24–28 days.

Description: This unmistakable woodpecker (16") is largely black with a red crest and a white stripe on the face and neck. There is also white in the wing linings and at the base of the primaries that show when it flies The male also has a red "moustache" mark.

Distribution: Broadly distributed in forested habitat across North America except for the southern Rocky Mountains. In Crater Lake National

Pileated Woodpecker, male

Pileated Woodpecker, male

Park they are relatively common in Shasta fir, white fir, and Douglas-fir stands. They are less common at higher elevations but occur year-round.

American Kestrel
Falco sparverius

When the montane meadows fill with grasshoppers in late summer, American Kestrels are there to greet them. Kestrels follow available prey into the mountains as the retreating snow releases plants to grow and bloom in the meadows. In turn, this burst in productivity provides food for grasshoppers and a host of other insects. Grasshoppers are easy to catch, relatively speaking, and provide a rich energy source. Kestrels also prey on small rodents, reptiles, and even small birds when the opportunity presents itself.

While many falcons are active hunters, pursuing quick and agile prey, Kestrels are "sit-and-wait" predators. They prefer to sit quietly from an elevated perch, scanning the ground for prey before pouncing. However, if a steady breeze is blowing, they may take wing, face the wind, and hover. This allows them to search new areas with additional prey, areas lacking opportunities for perch hunting. They may even hover on windless days, but it is harder work.

These small falcons are brightly colored, unusual for a bird of prey. Unlike many raptors, males and females differ in the color and pattern of their plumage. They also differ in other ways. In winter males and females tend to use different habitats. Males inhabit open country with minimal vegetative cover, while females tend to inhabit more cluttered habitats with denser vegetation.

Kestrels regularly harass Red-tailed Hawks and other potential predators, often using their distinctive "killi-killi-killi" call. American Kestrels nest in cavities, often the old nests of Northern Flickers. Like all falcons, they construct no nest. The female lays 4–5 eggs richly marked in reddish-brown. Incubation takes 30 days, and the young fledge in 28–31 days.

Description: This small falcon (9"–12") is slightly larger than an American Robin. Both male and female have a dark "tear" mark beneath the eye that is characteristic of falcons. The wings of the male are bluish-gray while wings of the female are reddish-brown with dark bands. The underparts of the male are pale orange with a variable spotting, and the underparts of the female are streaked. The tails, too, differ. The male has a bright orange tail with a black band near the tip; the female has a reddish-brown tail with narrow dark bands.

American Kestrel, male

American Kestrel, female

Distribution: American Kestrels occur from Alaska to Argentina. Locally they frequent farm country, grasslands, and other open habitat on both sides of the Cascades. Kestrels are sparse breeders at lower elevations in the southern portion of the park.

Peregrine Falcon
Falco peregrinus

A crow-sized raptor with pointed wings and a bluish-gray back soars below the rim. The Peregrine Falcon plays in the wind, waiting for the time to hunt. From its aerie on the walls of the rim, it may travel many miles to favored hunting areas, possibly as far as the marshes around Upper Klamath Lake. Falcons will travel 15 miles or more from the nest.

When seeking prey, the Peregrine employs a hunting strategy that differs from many of its close relatives. Rather than using the low-level pursuit preferred by Prairie Falcons, it soars high, waiting for a bird to fly over the canopy of the forest or above the reeds of a marsh. Once a bird is in the open, the falcon dives. With few flicks of the wings, the falcon accelerates to more than 100 miles per hour. When it pulls out of its dive, it quickly overtakes its fleeing prey, grabbing it in its talons if small or slashing it with the talons of its hind toes or stunning it with balled foot if larger. At these speeds it must be careful not to injure itself.

The Peregrine Falcon suffered greatly from the use of pesticides just as did the Bald Eagle, Osprey, and Brown Pelican. The birds that make up the diet of the falcon accumulated pesticides just as did the fish that are the prey of the others. The last remaining breeding Peregrine Falcons in Oregon in the 1960s and 1970s were at Crater Lake. With curtailment in the use of DDT, they have quickly recovered and again nest within the park and many other places in Oregon as well.

They prey almost entirely on flying birds, anywhere in size from finches to ducks. A bird that refuses to fly is usually safe. They build no nest of their own but use the old nests of other birds such as ravens or lay their eggs in rocky recesses. The chosen nest site is usually protected from above because other raptors, including Great Horned Owls, occasionally prey on them. They lay 3–5 reddish brown eggs. The period of incubation is 33–35 days, and the young fledge when about 6 weeks old.

Description: The Peregrine Falcon is a medium-sized falcon (16"). It has long pointed wings and a moderately long tail. The back is steely blue, and the belly is creamy white with spots varying in extent among individuals. The dark hood distinguishes it from its browner cousin, the Prairie Falcon, which sometimes visits the park after the breeding season. Prairie Falcons breed to the east in the high desert.

Peregrine Falcon

Peregrine Falcon

Distribution: Peregrine Falcons are found on every continent except Antarctica, and they breed in many habitats, from remote rocky coasts to the tall buildings and bridges of large cities. In winter, northern populations in North America migrate to central and South America. Coastal birds may remain on territory year-round. In Crater Lake National Park, the rim offers the best chance to view these birds.

Olive-sided Flycatcher

Contopus cooperi

Olive-sided Flycatchers are characteristically found on an exposed perch, often on the top of a dead tree at the edge of a meadow. The short bushy crest gives it a large-headed look. It waits patiently, scanning the sky for flying insects, and dashes out to pluck a passing wasp from the air with a snap of the beak, returning to the same perch. It may subdue the prey with a whack on the branch before swallowing the prize. Again and again, it sallies out and returns to the same perch in the manner typical of many flycatchers.

The Olive-sided Flycatcher is not a common flycatcher, but if there is one in the area, you will soon know. Its song is loud and may carry a quarter of a mile or more. To many the song sounds like "Quick! Three beers!" This is the first song many beginning birders learn because it is so clear and distinctive.

Flycatchers are relatively primitive perching birds, and unlike their relatives including robins, warblers, and sparrows, they do not learn their song. It is written somewhere in their DNA. An Olive-sided Flycatcher that has never heard another sing will sing a perfect "Quick! Three Beers!" upon reaching its territory in its first breeding year.

They prefer forest edges and habitat that permits a clear view for some distance. For reasons that are not clear, this species has declined in abundance in recent years throughout its range. The decline is somewhat surprising, given that forest management practices create abundant edge habitat.

The female typically constructs a small cup-shaped nest composed of plant fibers and grasses placed on a bare horizontal limb. The 3 lightly spotted eggs hatch in about 2 weeks, and both parents feed the young. The young fledge in 19–21 days, giving them just a few weeks to refine their hunting skills before taking off on the long journey to South America, one of the longest journeys of any small bird breeding in western forests.

Description: Olive-sided Flycatchers (7.5") are dull green with a relatively large head and a short bushy crest and a short tail. Olive-green patches on its sides give it the appearance that it is wearing a vest. It has two white wing bars and often two distinct white patches low on its back. Male and female are similar.

Olive-sided Flycatcher

Olive-sided Flycatcher

Distribution: Breeds broadly in North America from Canada to Mexico. In Crater Lake National Park it is a regular but uncommon breeder from timberline down. It arrives in early May and departs by early September, wintering in the upper Amazon Basin in winter.

Hammond's Flycatcher, Dusky Flycatcher, and Western Flycatcher

Empidonax hammondii, E. wrightii, and E. difficilis

Some of the most frustrating birds to identify are the small flycatchers. Dull green in color, they sport a short bushy crest, two white wing bars, and usually a narrow eye ring. Most tend to flick their tail as they scan the air and vegetation for prey. An honest birder will often confess to being uncertain as to which species they have seen.

Sometimes they are simply referred to as "LGBs" or little green birds. Other birders refer to them as "empidonaxes," for their scientific name. They differ subtly in bill form and color, general body color, and the amount of white around the eye. They also differ in their calls and song, but it takes experience to make an accurate identification this way. Even then there's room for argument among serious birders. The best clue is often habitat and call. Of the three species inhabiting the park, the Dusky Flycatcher lives in the driest habitats, usually containing shrubs. The Western Flycatcher lives at lower elevations, most often in Douglas-fir and along the streams. The Hammond's Flycatcher lives in the deepest forests and at higher elevations than the other two.

Like the Olive-sided Flycatcher, these flycatchers tend to perch upright and wait for passing flying insects. However, they perch much lower, often beneath the forest canopy or at the brush tops, depending on the species. They also fly out to grab insects from vegetation.

Each weaves a small cup-shaped nest of plant fibers that is concealed within the vegetation. They lay 3–4 lightly spotted white eggs. Incubation and fledging periods each last just over 2 weeks, and both parents feed the young.

Description: All three species are small greenish birds (5.5") with two white wing bars. They are much smaller than the Olive-sided Flycatcher, being the size of a small sparrow. The Hammond's Flycatcher is the smallest and darkest, with a shorter bill and tail than the other two. The small bill of the Hammond's Flycatcher is almost entirely black. The Western Flycatcher has a belly that is more yellow and a broader white eye ring than the other two, while the Dusky Flycatcher is duller and has a slightly longer bill and tail.

Distribution: All occur in their preferred habitat in western North America during the breeding season and retreat to Mexico and Central

Hammond's Flycatcher

Dusky Flycatcher

Western Flycatcher

America for the winter. In the park they arrive in May and depart by late September.

Western Warbling Vireo

Vireo swainsoni

From deep in the vegetation along Annie Creek, a bold, clear but abrupt song is repeated endlessly in the early summer heat. The Western Warbling Vireo, a plain-colored bird, is more often heard than seen. The song is one of the defining songs of riparian habitat throughout the state and much of North America and often finds its way on to soundtracks of movies when a background of spring birdsong is called for.

Like all vireos, it forages deliberately, often spending 30 seconds or more on a single perch before moving on. The Western Warbling Vireo moves its head from side to side and up and down as it carefully scans the foliage of willows and aspen for caterpillars and other invertebrates. In this way it seeks out larger but rarer prey than many other insectivorous birds in the same habitat. This helps them avoid competition with gleaners that move more rapidly through the vegetation.

The nest of the Western Warbling Vireo is a work of art, constructed of spider silk and fine vegetation situated in the fork of a limb. Decorated with lichens and bits of vegetation, it hangs like a cup from its rim. This manner of construction is a trait exhibited by all vireos.

Western Warbling Vireos typically lay 4 eggs with an incubation period of 12–13 days and a fledgling period of 12–14 days. In other areas they are frequent hosts to the eggs and young of Brown-headed Cowbirds. Cowbirds are brood parasites that lay their eggs in the nests of other birds, frequently leading to the loss of the host's young. Fortunately, cowbirds are rare in the park.

There is a second vireo at Crater Lake National Park, although not common. The Cassin's Vireo wears white spectacles and white wing bars that distinguish it from the Western Warbling Vireo. It is not a riparian species but instead inhabits coniferous forests at lower elevations. The Cassin's Vireo song consists of brief phrases sounding like a bird asking and answering its own questions. One brief phrase ends with an upward inflection and the next phrase falls.

Description: Western Warbling Vireos are small (5.5") light brown birds with a bill somewhat larger than that of a warbler. The undersides are off-white, and about the only distinguishing mark is a pale line over the eye. Male and female are similar.

Distribution: Western Warbling Vireos occur across North America

Western Warbling Vireo

Western Warbling Vireo

from northern Canada to Mexico. They winter in Central America. At Crater Lake National Park they are an uncommon breeding bird in the riparian vegetation along the lower reaches of the creeks, including Annie Creek, arriving in early May and departing by early September.

Canada Jay
Perisoreus canadensis

Whiskey jack! Camp robber! These are just a couple of the names this tame jay has acquired. Canada Jays are birds of the high country, usually confined to the white fir and noble fir forests of the Cascades. Deep snow and bitter cold are not enough to force a family of these jays from their familiar portion of the forest. Their relative, the Steller's Jay, is quicker to retreat to lower elevations in the quest for slightly warmer weather and more abundant food.

Sometimes this bird is overly friendly, helping itself to food left insufficiently attended on a picnic table. They are largely silent birds and seek out noises in the woods such as a fallen tree or sounds of a predator in hopes that it may mean a free meal. They have a fondness for fatty foods, those rich in energy, and will even take a slice of sizzling bacon right out of the frying pan.

Sometimes hikers have had the ominous feeling that they are being followed, imagining large and threatening creatures. Very often it means that a Canada Jay or more often a pair or family is quietly trailing the hikers as they walk through the forest. A hiker may be startled to find a jay is perched just a few feet behind their shoulder. Before humans frequented the area, they followed predators, picking over the remains of a deer or other prey left behind. This comes in handy in the dark and cold winter months when food is hard to come by in the high country. They spend much of the summer caching food for the lean times.

Canada Jays are not particular about what they eat. Insects, seeds, fruits, carrion, and even potato chips are suitable fare, but please don't feed them. Their cup-shaped nest composed of small twigs is difficult to locate. They lay 3–4 eggs, which hatch in 18–19 days. Young are fed by both parents and fledge in about 23 days.

Description: Canada Jays are relatively small (11.5") and have a gray body. The head is largely white with a dark gray patch extending from eye to eye around the back of the head. Young birds are uniformly dark gray but acquire adult plumage by the end of their first summer. Male and female are similar.

Distribution: Canada Jays occur in boreal forests across Alaska and Canada and in western North America as far south as northern California. In addition to those in the high country, a darker form inhabits the deep

Canada Jay

Canada Jay

forests along the coast. Family groups are a common sight throughout the park in all forest types and at all times of the year.

Steller's Jay
Cyanocitta stelleri

From deep in the forest a harsh call breaks the silence. The Steller's Jay is far more vocal than the Canada Jay. Vocalizations range from a variety of harsh and grating calls to less discordant calls to a very soft and melodic subsong heard only at very close range and then only rarely. It is a dark blue jay with a black hood and crest, and some people mistakenly call it a "Blue Jay." It is a jay, and it is blue, but the true Blue Jay is a bird of the eastern hardwood forests and not an Oregon bird.

Steller's Jays were named after the German naturalist Georg Steller. Steller traveled with the Dane, Vitus Bering, as they explored Alaska for Russia in 1741. Steller's Eiders, Steller's Sea Eagles, Steller's sea lions, and Steller's sea cows are other animals named for this naturalist. The sea cow, a former resident of the Aleutian Islands, is now extinct.

Family groups of Steller's Jays remain together through the fall and winter as they forage slowly and systematically throughout the forest, checking out every potential source of food from canopy to forest floor. They are omnivorous, feeding on almost anything with food value, from insects to seeds to fruits to the eggs and nestlings of other birds. They have even been observed harvesting tiny fish along the shore, flipping them onto the bank where they are easily gathered up.

Steller's Jays are mimics. However, unlike Mockingbirds, Starlings, and Lesser Goldfinches that imitate a wide range of sounds, from tree frogs to Wood Ducks, Steller's Jays mimic the calls of hawks including both Red-tailed and Red-shouldered hawks. Why they tend to mimic just these birds is unclear. The calls of hawks share some of the same sound characteristics with jays, and it may be the only calls they can imitate. Others have wondered whether they mimic hawks to startle competitors, especially squirrels, thereby gaining greater access to food.

Steller's Jays build a stick nest lined with mud low in a tree and lay 3–5 turquoise blue eggs heavily marked in brown. Both members of the pair incubate the eggs for about 16 days, and the young fledge in about 17–18 days.

Description: A medium-sized bird (11.5") with navy blue body, wings, and tail. The head and back are black. They also have small blue or white marks on their forehead. Primaries and tail are finely barred in black. Male and female are similar.

Steller's Jay

Steller's Jay

Distribution: Steller's Jays occur in montane forests from southeastern Alaska through Mexico. They are a common breeding bird throughout the park, though many retreat to warmer habitats at lower elevations in the park in winter.

Clark's Nutcracker
Nucifraga columbiana

If there is one species that most people associate with Crater Lake National Park, it is the Clark's Nutcracker. More likely than not it is the first bird a visitor sees at the rim. Perhaps a family group flies from the top of a whitebark pine, taking off on black wings looking as if it lacked a tail. The white tail and secondary flight feathers often disappear against the mountain sky. If you are sitting on a rock wall enjoying the view of the lake, maybe a nutcracker silently lands nearby hoping for a peanut or other item of food. Please resist the impulse to feed them. It is a national park and feeding wild animals is illegal. While you are lining up a picture of Wizard Island from the Watchman, a loud and raspy call rings out in the mountain air. An unseen nutcracker is perched in a tree below the rim. At the Pinnacles, a family of nutcrackers may forage among the huge cones hanging from the drooping tips of the spreading limbs of the sugar pines. They are everywhere, birds looking for mischief, perhaps inserting themselves into every picture taken from the rim. They have little fear of people.

Clark's Nutcrackers specialize on the seeds of conifers, especially those of the whitebark pine. Individual birds may cache 10,000 seeds or more of whitebark pine, buried in the ground in small caches or tucked away among the branches of a tree. Like all crows and jays, they also feed on a wide variety of other foods, including insects and other seeds. Their nest is composed of small sticks and placed high in a conifer. They rear 3–5 young that fledge in about three weeks. Incubation is about 18–22 days.

Description: The Clark's Nutcracker is a gray bird about the size and shape of a small crow (12"). The face is white and the wings are black. The wings have a large white panel, and the tail is largely white. Male and female are similar.

Distribution: Clark's Nutcrackers are regular inhabitants of the forests near timberline throughout western North America. They also occur at somewhat lower elevations in ponderosa pine forests and even juniper woodlands. The Clark's Nutcrackers of Crater Lake National Park appear to nest at lower elevations and arrive at the rim after their young have fledged. They remain into the fall, feeding on whitebark pine seeds, but most depart for other areas in winter. Birds banded in the park have been seen as far away as Mount Adams.

Clark's Nutcracker

Clark's Nutcracker

Common Raven
Corvus corax

Crows are too civilized to live in the park. They frequent farmland and cities. They require more benign climates. They are comfortable in flocks composed of dozens. The Common Raven, in contrast, more often lives far from human activities. They thrive among the summits, riding the winds that rise off the cliffs and curl over the edge of the rim. Winter snow and wind seem not to bother these birds. The conditions simply offer new opportunities. Where crows merely fly from point A to point B on labored wings, ravens consider the skies their playground. They soar with hawks and harass them as much for play as to protect their young. Pairs engage in synchronized flights that involve impressive chases with twists and turns, snap rolls, and dives. They are also smart and inquisitive, quick to check out anything new in their realm. Unlike crows, ravens rarely gather in flocks. Instead, they travel alone or in pairs or, later in the summer, in family groups.

Ravens eat a wide variety of foods, from newly sprouted wheat to garbage to roadkill, and are capable of successfully hunting lizards, rabbits, and squirrels on their own, often hunting cooperatively as a pair. Some ecologists consider them to be raptors along with hawks, eagles, falcons, and owls because of their lifestyle. In winter, scavenging is an important food source, and they may gather at the remains of a deer brought down by other predators or killed by a car. They nest most often on cliffs, building a tidy stick nest usually sheltered from above. Golden Eagles and Great Horned Owls are threats to the incubating female and young. A typical brood is 5–7 young. Incubation is about 3 weeks, and the young fledge in about 4–7 weeks.

Description: The Common Raven is large (24") and glossy black. They differ from crows in several ways. They are larger, and the bill of the raven is proportionately larger. Also, the feathers about the neck are shaggy, and the tail is longer and wedge-shaped (the tail of the crow is square). The wings are longer and narrower, and their calls are also very different. Ravens have a variety of calls including croaks, harsh squawks, and chortles rather than the simple "caw" of a crow.

Distribution: Common Ravens are widespread in North America, absent from only the prairie states and the forests of the southeast. They occur from coast to mountaintop but are less common in agricultural

Common Raven

Common Raven

lands and in cities. They also occur across Europe and Asia. At Crater
Lake National Park they occur everywhere except the deepest forests
and often hang around the edges of human activities. Many may leave
the park in winter, but some remain year-round.

Mountain Chickadee
Poecile gambeli

A quiet "chick-a-dee-dee" call filters down from high in a lodgepole pine. A single bird is absorbed as it works hard to extract a pupa from deep within a curl of bark. It sounds like the familiar Black-capped Chickadee found along the creeks in the valleys at lower elevations and occasionally in the park, but the call is harsher. The high country chickadee is the Mountain Chickadee, inhabiting true firs, lodgepole pines, and mountain hemlocks. To the east, the range of the Mountain Chickadee continues out into the ponderosa pine forest and older stands of juniper woodland.

The Mountain Chickadee, having successfully retrieved its prize from the tree bark, calls once more and flies off to another tree. Only then is it apparent that it is not alone. A second bird follows, then another. In all, a small troop of eight or so birds works its way through the forest, sometimes in the treetops and at others low in the understory. Mountain Chickadees typically travel in family groups, occasionally calling to maintain contact. Only during the breeding season is it common to see pairs or individual birds.

As they travel through the forest, they scrutinize every crack in the bark, every clump of lichens and every bud for insect eggs and spiders. They frequently hang upside down in their quest, giving them a perspective untapped by others. Besides invertebrates, Mountain Chickadees eat a variety of foods including seeds and fruits when available. They have even been observed to glean bits of fat and flesh from the abandoned carcass of a deer left behind by scavengers or to collect items from the ground.

Their song differs from their "chick-a-dee" call and is heard in the spring and summer. To many the song sounds as if they are saying "cheese-bur-ger."

They nest in a cavity in a tree, either an old nest excavated by a woodpecker or a natural cavity, or even one of their own creation, usually in wood softened by rot. Being a cavity nester, where the risk of predation is less, they rear more young than other birds of similar size with open-cup nests, usually from 5–9 young. Incubation is about 2 weeks and the young fledge when about 3 weeks of age.

Another chickadee, the Chestnut-backed Chickadee, lives among Douglas-fir at middle- and lower elevations to the west and can be readily

Mountain Chickadee

Mountain Chickadee

observed along Red Blanket Creek in the southwest corner of the park.

Description: Mountain Chickadees are small (5.25") gray birds with a black cap and throat bordering the white face. The bill is small, and the tail is relatively long. Unlike other chickadees, they also have a white line over the eye. Male and female are similar.

Distribution: Mountain Chickadees occur in the mountains from British Columbia to southern Arizona and New Mexico. Unlike many breeding birds in the park that head south or drop to lower elevations in winter, the Mountain Chickadee remains throughout the year, inhabiting most forest types.

Horned Lark
Eremophila alpestris

In early spring in the open rangeland east of the Cascades, listen for a high-pitched song that sounds somewhat like glass wind chimes. To search for the singer, don't look among the bunchgrasses or the tops of sage. Look higher. The Horned Lark sings most often while flying high above its territory. Once finished, it drops to the ground and resumes foraging. For a grassland bird they have relatively short legs, making it difficult for them to clamber among dense tufts of grass and other vegetation. Instead, they prefer habitat with abundant bare ground, where they search for small seeds and insects.

The high country provides habitat similar in structure to much of the open country east of the Cascades. Subalpine areas are characterized by widely scattered plants with much bare ground in between. While not abundant at higher elevation in the Cascades, scattered populations of Horned Larks can be found on some of the peaks. A small population was discovered on Llao Rock in the 1930s. Small populations of most species tend to persist for a short while before disappearing, maybe to reappear at a later date. The population on Llao Rock is not visited by ornithologists every year, but the population appears quite durable and is still active. A great many species of larks are found throughout the Old World, but only one, the Horned Lark, occurs in North America.

The nest is tightly woven and concealed carefully among the subalpine plants. They rear two or more broods of 2–5 young at lower elevations but likely raise just a single brood along the rim of Crater Lake, where the growing season is quite brief. The incubation period is 11 days, and the young fledge in about 10 days.

Description: The brown sparrow-sized bird (7.25") has a thin bill. At close range you can see the yellow face, the black crescent on the chest, and maybe even the thin black "horns" on its head. More often it is observed as it flushes from the rocky soils and retreats to quieter places. The combination of white outer tail feathers, black central tail feathers, and a rosy brown back will help you identify this bird as it disappears from view. Males and females are similar.

Distribution: Horned Larks occur across North America in open habitats ranging from tundra to prairie to coastal dunes. They winter in the southern United States and northern Mexico. At Crater Lake they breed

Horned Lark

Horned Lark

on Llao Rock and occasionally the Pumice Desert, arriving soon after the meadows are free of snow and leave by the end of August.

Violet-green Swallow

Tachycenita thalassina

Swallows of several species are abundant over the marshes, fields, and rivers just outside the park, but only one regularly makes the park its summer home. The Violet-green Swallow frequents the steep slopes below the rim and in the canyons in the southern portion of the park, where you might first notice them by the flash of their white belly or staccato two- to three-note call. Some even nest in rocky recesses in the Phantom Ship. Their flight path is anything but straight as they twist and weave through the air in pursuit of small flying insects. They remind some of slalom skiers as they fly. Cold, wet weather makes it difficult for swallows. Insects fly little when it rains or the wind is blowing. At these times the swallows congregate low over streams and lakes, where the few insects braving the weather are apparently available. On calm, sunny days, you may hear their calls only from high above as they pursue their prey.

Other swallows you may encounter on occasion in the park include Cliff, Barn, and Northern Rough-winged Swallows. They may be seen over the mountain meadows and along the ridges in passage in late summer as they head south for the winter.

The seven swallows in Oregon feed almost exclusively on flying insects. Swallows construct three different types of nests. Some nest in tree or other natural cavities like the Violet-green Swallow. Others build mud nests attached to cliffs or buildings, including the Barn and Cliff Swallows. The third create a burrow into a mud bank along a stream or river, as does the Northern Rough-winged Swallow. Clutches range from 4–6 eggs. Incubation lasts 14–15 days. Both parents feed the young for the 23–24 days they remain in the nest. Cavity nesters of many species typically have larger broods and remain in the nest for an extended period.

Description: Most swallows are small birds with long wings and small bills. The Violet-green Swallow (5.25") has a green back and cap with violet highlights on the upper tail coverts and a white belly. It differs from the other greenish swallow, the Tree Swallow, by its white rump patches and small white patch around the eyes.

Distribution: The Violet-green Swallow breeds throughout western North America. It arrives early (March) and stays late (October). Most winter along the coast of western Mexico. Others, including Barn and Cliff Swallows, head farther south. In the park, Violet-green Swallows

Violet-green Swallow

Violet-green Swallow

occur in the narrow canyons along Annie, Sun, and Sand Creeks and along the steep walls inside the rim of the crater.

Ruby-crowned Kinglet
Corthylio calendula

Hiking near timberline, you might hear a loud and rich song that starts slowly and builds from within a small conifer. Don't be surprised if the singer is a tiny yellow-green bird with a tiny red patch on the top of its head. The song seems far too large to come from such a tiny bird. Except when singing, courting, or challenging a rival, the red crown of the male is usually concealed.

Not many Ruby-crowned Kinglets breed in the park. They are more common during migration and abandon the ark entirely during the winter except for maybe a few among the willows along the lower reaches of Annie Creek.

Although related to the Golden-crowned Kinglet, the Ruby-crowned Kinglet differs in several important ways. Ruby-crowned Kinglets forage much closer to the ground, usually less than 20' up, while Golden-crowned Kinglets tend to remain high in the canopy. Ruby-crowned Kinglets are solitary foragers most of the time, while Golden-crowned Kinglets tend to forage in family groups. Their manner of foraging is similar though. They move rapidly from perch to perch through the limbs and foliage, gleaning minute eggs from a stem or an aphid from a leaf or a small pupa from a crack in the bark. Sometimes they hover briefly to pluck a tiny insect from the very end of a branch. While Ruby-crowned Kinglets feed primarily on insects, they will also visit the sap wells of sapsuckers and bird feeders provisioned with suet during the winter.

As they forage, they occasionally flick their wings in a manner often characterized as "nervous." This behavior is not shared with the Golden-crowned Kinglet. Other species that flick their wings or tail, such as American Redstarts, do so to startle and flush potential prey. It is likely the same explanation applies to the Ruby-crowned Kinglet.

The staccato two-note call is distinctive. Their nest is a woven cup concealed among the foliage, where they rear 5–9 young. The period of incubation is 14 days, and the young fledge after 16 days.

Description: The Ruby-crowned Kinglet is a small (4.25") dull greenish bird with a short tail and tiny bill. It has two white wing bars and a narrow white eye ring. The male has a tiny red patch on the top of the head raised for display either in courtship or the defense of territory.

Ruby-crowned Kinglet, male

Ruby-crowned Kinglet, male

Distribution: During the breeding season, they inhabit coniferous forests across Canada and United States. In winter they retreat to the southern United States, where they frequent woodlands, hedgerows, and thickets. In Crater Lake National Park they are a sparse summer resident, most common among the lodgepole pines.

Golden-crowned Kinglet

Regulus satrapa

Hold a nickel and a penny on one hand and a Golden-crowned Kinglet in the other. The two coins weigh more than the bird. It is almost beyond understanding that a warm-blooded bird this small can survive in the harsh environmental conditions in the park in winter. Yet, it is perhaps the most abundant bird in the park, summer or winter.

If you pause along any of the forest trails and listen, you may hear the contact calls of this bird, some clear in tone and some characteristically "burry." The notes are too high in pitch for many to hear.

These birds are always on the move, flitting from branch to branch, inspecting a bud at the end of a thin branch or hovering in front of a cluster of needles on an endless search for tiny insects, spiders, eggs, and pupa. They typically feed high in the canopy but at times may be found at all levels within the forest.

Most of the year they travel in flocks composed of one or more families. It is not unusual to find more than 40 birds in a single flock, though 6–20 is more common. At close range you might hear a variety of soft mutterings. The soft calls help to keep a family group together as they feed, and they are frequently accompanied by chickadees, nuthatches, and creepers. With so many eyes in a flock, predators find it difficult to approach a flock unaware. Only during the breeding season do the birds disperse.

The song is very high-pitched, like their calls. It begins slowly with repeated notes and cascades into a jumble of rapidly delivered notes. The nest is a small woven cup placed high in a conifer, where they lay from 5–10 eggs. The young hatch in 15 days and fledge in another 18–19 days. **Description:** It is a small greenish bird (4") with a short tail and tiny bill. At very close range, if you are fortunate, you will see the black and white stripes on its head with a yellow crown, tinged with orange in the male. They have two white wing bars.

Distribution: Golden-crowned Kinglets breed in boreal forests across North America. In winter they disperse from the northern portions of their range and spread to almost all forest types. In the park this bird is most common among the true firs and Douglas-firs, scarce in the ponderosa pines, and nearly absent in riparian areas and other deciduous trees.

Golden-crowned Kinglet, male

Golden-crowned Kinglet, female

Red-breasted Nuthatch
Sitta canadensis

To watch a Red-breasted Nuthatch is to watch an acrobat completely at ease in its three-dimensional world. It may hang from the tip of the outermost limb one moment and then scoot along the underside of a large limb, completely unaware it is defying gravity. Finally, it strikes out headfirst down the trunk of the tree, scouring the bark for hidden insects or spider eggs or seeds that have fallen into a crack. Foraging headfirst down a trunk is the signature move of all nuthatches. This ability gives them a perspective that other birds such as woodpeckers do not have, and the resources that come with it. Woodpeckers have a stiff tail that they use for support and to help them move in a vertical world, but it only helps going up. The tail of a nuthatch, in contrast, is short and unsuitable as a prop. Instead, strong oversized feet are the secret to its success.

Red-breasted Nuthatches, like many small forest birds, travel in small family groups, often joining the larger groups of chickadees and kinglets in winter. Their call is as distinctive as their behavior, and often the first clue that they are in the area. It is a nasal "yank, yank, yank" that reminds some people of the beeping of a delivery truck backing up. They do not appear to have a song separate from their call notes.

Red-breasted Nuthatches nest in cavities, either old cavities excavated by a woodpecker or one they make themselves. Curiously, they frequently smear pitch around the entrance to the nest. This may serve to discourage potential predators. A typical clutch is 4–7 eggs with an incubation period of about 12–13 days. The young fledge in about 3 weeks.

There are three species of nuthatches in Oregon, and each has its favored habitat. The largest is the White-breasted Nuthatch that inhabits white oaks and, to a lesser extent, ponderosa pine. The smallest is the Pygmy Nuthatch that lives almost exclusively in ponderosa pine. Red-breasted Nuthatches tend to avoid ponderosa pines, but frequent most other conifers including true firs, Douglas-fir, western hemlock, and coast redwood.

Description: The Red-breasted Nuthatch (4.5") has a gray back and orange underparts. A bright white line over the eye separates the black cap and line through the eye of the male. The cap of the female is a sooty gray rather than black.

Red-breasted Nuthatch

Red-breasted Nuthatch

Distribution: Red-breasted Nuthatches inhabit a wide range of coniferous forests in Canada and the United States. In winter they expand their range unpredictably into towns and hardwood forests. It may be common in an area one winter and then absent for the next four. At Crater Lake National Park they occur in all forest types, except ponderosa pines. They remain in the park year-round, but numbers diminish in winter.

Brown Creeper
Certhia americana

A small bark-colored bird with a thin curved bill clings vertically to the trunk and silently works its way up the tree in an endless quest for food. It disappears around the back of the tree only to reappear on the other side higher up. In this manner, it may continue to the highest reaches in the tree. Finished with one tree, it flies to the base of a neighboring tree and begins a new search, spiraling up. This is the Brown Creeper. No other bird in the region is similar in appearance or behavior, and they have no close relatives in North America.

Their tail is remarkably like that of a woodpecker's, with stiff pointed shafts that serve as support as they work their way up the trunks. Also like woodpeckers, the central two tail feathers, which are the strongest, do not molt until all the other tail feathers have been fully replaced, ensuring their ability to forage throughout the year. They are committed to "creeping" up trunks and appear unable to perch crosswise on a branch in the manner of other small birds.

Brown Creepers tend to forage alone or in pairs, unlike many small birds of the forest canopy that travel in family groups when not rearing young. However, they will often tag along with the mixed flocks of chickadees, kinglets, and other birds during the winter. There is safety in numbers.

They are a quiet bird, with a short, high-pitched song. Their song varies geographically and, in this region, sounds to some like "trees, trees, beautiful trees." They also occasionally give a short, clear, high-pitched note that helps them stay in contact with others when they forage.

Brown Creepers feed exclusively on insects gleaned from the branches and trunks of trees. The nest of the Brown Creeper, appropriately enough, is constructed behind a piece of loose bark on the trunk of a tree, where they rear from 5–7 young. Incubation lasts 15 days, and the young fledge at about 16 days of age.

Description: The Brown Creeper (5.25") perches vertically on tree trunks. It is striped, brown above and white below. The long thin bill is decurved, and it has a stiff pointed tail that supports the bird as is climbs. A tan stripe shows in the wing when it flies, and the sexes are similar.

Distribution: Brown Creepers occur in coniferous forests from the Appalachians to the Pacific Coast and from Canada to Mexico. They are

Brown Creeper

Brown Creeper

equally at home in the gallery forests of cottonwoods along streams and rivers. In the park it is widespread, occupying most forest types but never in abundance. In winter, one to a few may accompany family flocks of chickadees or kinglets as they forage.

Rock Wren
Salpinctes obsoletus

There is a wren for nearly every habitat. The aptly named Marsh Wren inhabits the reed beds in the refuges of the Klamath Basin. The House Wren frequents backyards and oak woodlands. In the desert Southwest, the Cactus Wren finds its home among the saguaros. Even the boulder-strewn slopes inside the rim of Crater Lake have their wren, the Rock Wren. Wrens, in general, are known for their spirit, exuberant songs, and a tail held high. The Rock Wren is no exception.

While enjoying the view of Crater Lake from Cloudcap or the Watchman, listen for the clear ringing call of the Rock Wren from the slopes below. As it forages, the energetic sandy brown bird disappears among the rocks. Emerging a short distance away, it quickly scans for predators, calls, and disappears again. It weaves among the boulders, negotiating the narrowest of cracks, searching above, below, and in between for tiny insects. The long thin slightly decurved bill is ideal for probing deep crevices. After feeding it may perch quietly on an exposed rock, basking in the mountain sun, keeping watch over its territory.

To the east in the high desert it lives with its cousin, the Canyon Wren. Where the Rock Wren lives among the rubble at the foot of a cliff, the Canyon Wren lives among the crevices high on the cliff walls. The Rock Wren is a migratory species while the Canyon Wren is sedentary. This may explain why, of the two species, only the Rock Wren is found in the park. The deep snow of a Crater Lake winter makes it impossible for either to remain.

The neatly woven nest of the Rock Wren is typically tucked away under a rock. For reasons that are unclear, the female lines a pathway to the nest with small pebbles. The clutch of 5–6 eggs is incubated for 12 days before hatching. Young fledge in 14–16 days.

Description: The Rock Wren (6") is a sandy-colored bird with a long thin bill and tan corners to its long tail. The tail is frequently held high over the back like most wrens. Male and female are similar in appearance.

Distribution: Rock Wrens breed throughout the Intermountain West from April to October. As fall approaches, Rock Wrens head to the southwestern United States and northern Mexico to wait for the spring melt. At Crater Lake they breed in the talus slopes above the lake and other outcrops and rocky areas.

Rock Wren

Rock Wren

Pacific Wren
Troglodytes pacificus

In the dark forest understory, amid the tangle of down logs and moss-covered limbs, an enthusiastic song rings out, filling the gloom. The endless notes pour out in rapid succession continuing for ten seconds, then twenty seconds, and more, seldom repeating a phrase, rising and falling in pitch and changing cadence many times before falling into silence. If one is patient, the bird will continue its solo performance several times before taking a break to feed. It is difficult to catch the singer in the act. Later, however, a tiny brown bird may reveal its presence and scurry along the ground and among the fallen limbs and tangled roots much like a mouse. If it takes notice of your presence, it may rise to the top of a log and challenge with sharp call notes, usually doubled. The minute bird with the seemingly huge lungs is a Pacific Wren.

Like all wrens, it has a thin bill for gleaning and plucking insects from cracks and crevices and a tail that it holds high over its head. However, in comparison with most other wrens, it has the shortest of tails.

Pacific Wrens feed on a variety of insects and other small invertebrates. They construct a messy ball-like nest among a root tangle or in a cavity near the ground, where they rear as many as 7 young. Incubation lasts about 16–17 days, and the young spend another 16–17 days in the nest. Both parents incubate the eggs and care for the young.

The Pacific Wren was recently determined to be a separate species from both the Winter Wren of the boreal forests east of the Rocky Mountains and the Eurasian Wren of the Old World. Where the Pacific and Winter Wrens meet in British Columbia, the two sing different songs and do not interbreed.

Description: The Pacific Wren is a tiny dark brown bird (4") with wings and tail finely barred in black. The bill is thin, and the short tail is held high. Male and female are similar.

Distribution: Pacific Wrens occur in coniferous forests throughout the western United States and Canada. At Crater Lake National Park, Pacific Wrens inhabit dense forests, especially areas with low vegetation and woody debris. Most leave the park for less snowy areas in the winter and may be found in diverse habitats ranging from hedgerows to bramble patches.

Pacific Wren

Pacific Wren

American Dipper

Cinclus mexicanus

You might be chilling your feet in a rushing mountain stream when a small dark bird nearly the size of a robin alights on a rock in the middle of the swirling waters. It bobs its entire body a couple of times and plunges into the current. A few seconds later it pops to the surface for an instant, drifting with the stream, and then dives again. This time it climbs up on a rock with its beak full of mayfly and stonefly larvae. It bobs a couple of more times and then flies up the conifer-lined stream to its nest. This is the American Dipper, the only aquatic perching bird in North America. As long as the stream remains open, Dippers will continue to feed in these waters year-round.

Because they live in such a noisy environment, they rely on visual cues more than calls to remain in contact with mate and young. These cues include the frequent bobbing and blinking of the white eyelids that contrast with their slate-gray body.

Other adaptations include strong feet for clinging to the bottom of streams and small flaps of tissue that cover the nostrils when it dives. When it dives it typically faces upstream, head lowered, using the force of the stream to help hold it on the bottom while it searches for prey.

Dippers have a beautiful song that is thrush-like in character and delivered with the enthusiasm of a wren. However, it is seldom heard above the noise of the rushing stream. Its nest will be a bowl of moss constructed with a roof. The opening is on the side, like an oven, and will usually be placed behind a small waterfall where the splashing water will keep the moss moist and green. Bridges built close to the water are often accepted as a suitable substitute. A typical brood consists of 4–5 young. Incubation lasts 14–17 days, and the young fledge in about 24–26 days.

Description: Dippers (7.5") are uniformly sooty gray. They have a robin-like bill and a short upturned tail. Male and female are similar.

Distribution: Dippers inhabit fast-moving streams in the mountains of western Northern America from Alaska to Panama. They are largely nonmigratory. Dippers are found on most of the streams within the park. Watch for them along Annie Creek. At least one pair also breeds along the shore of Crater Lake, usually near Phantom Ship.

American Dipper

American Dipper

Mountain Bluebird
Sialia currucoides

It's impressive when a male Mountain Bluebird flies up and lands close on a low branch in a mountain meadow. Almost every feather is a dazzling turquoise blue, varying only in intensity, with the wings and tail brightest. If you are is quiet, it may patiently continue to scan the ground for caterpillars, grasshoppers, and other insects. It may fly out, hover, and then pounce. For much of the summer, Mountain Bluebirds remain in family groups, foraging in loose flocks. The females and young have only a touch of blue in wing and tail.

Bluebirds are early migrants and arrive at lower elevations in the park in April. The males arrive first, often as late winter storms are still adding snow at the rim. A flock of 10 or 20 male Mountain Bluebirds feeding quietly together in a meadow with a dusting of snow is an impressive sight. Its close relative the Western Bluebird occasionally visits the park but usually remains at lower elevations among the ponderosa pines.

Bluebirds are members of the thrush family. The family includes many like the nightingale that are excellent singers. The Hermit and Swainson's Thrushes that inhabit the park must be included on this list. The Mountain Bluebird, in contrast, has a simple song, barely worthy of mention. Apparently good looks are enough.

It is surprising to many to learn there are no blue pigments in the feathers of birds. Like the colors in the rainbow or the multicolored sheen in a soap bubble, the colors are structural, created by breaking light down to its component colors. In the case of bluebirds and jays, only the blue is free to return to our eyes. Grind a bluebird feather and the special structure within the feather is destroyed—all you will have is a brown powder.

They nest in the old nests of woodpeckers or other natural cavities. The 5–7 eggs are incubated for 13 days, and the young remain in the nest for 18–21 days.

Description: The male Mountain Bluebird (7.25") is unmistakable with its unmarked turquoise plumage. It is smaller than a robin, with a small bill and relatively long wings. The female is largely gray but still has traces of blue in the wing and tail.

Distribution: Mountain Bluebirds breed in drier habitats and at higher elevations in Western North America, being most common among

Mountain Bluebird, male

Mountain Bluebird, female

junipers. Most retreat to the southwestern United States and Mexico in winter. They breed widely in the park from the Panhandle to the rim, anywhere there are meadows or open woodland. They arrive in the park by May 1 and depart by late October.

Townsend's Solitaire
Myadestes townsendi

Along a forest trail in an area with little undergrowth, a silent gray bird with a long tail dashes out from its perch on a fallen log and grabs a passing insect. The white in the tail flashes briefly as it turns sharply and returns to its perch. It may sally out three or four times, sometimes as far as 30 feet before relocating to a new perch. Although the Townsend's Solitaire behaves like a flycatcher, it is a thrush, related to robins and bluebirds, and breeds widely in the park, but nowhere is it numerous. The best chance of observing one in the breeding season is among the ponderosa pines near the south entrance.

It has a loud and liquid song delivered from a high perch that can be heard from a great distance and lasts longer than those of most birds, but you will rarely catch a glimpse of the singer. They are shy and difficult to approach.

In winter they depart for lower elevations. Many head for the juniper woodlands east of the Cascades, where they maintain winter territories and can often be seen perched high. The "hollow" call note is soft and distinctive. On a rare February day when the sun is out and a touch of warmth is in the high-desert air, several birds may call from the tops of junipers. The calls have a ventriloquial quality, making it difficult to locate any single bird. With a dusting of snow on the ground insects are scarce, and at this time of year they feed largely on juniper berries. Juniper "berries" are actually cones, but the embedded bracts are fleshy and nutritious in comparison with the woody bracts of other conifer cones.

The nest is placed on or near the ground in a niche in a stump or fallen log. The 3–6 eggs are incubated for 12 days, and the young fledge in 10–14 days.

Description: Slightly smaller than a Robin, the trim Townsend's Solitaire (8.5") is gray with salmon-colored wing bars in the wing and white in the relatively long tail. The bill is small. Male and female are similar. Young birds are spotted below, a trait shared by all thrushes.

Distribution: Townsend's Solitaires breed throughout the mountains of western North America. In winter they shift southward, often becoming almost abundant among the junipers of central and eastern Oregon and points farther south. At Crater Lake, Townsend's Solitaires breed in open coniferous forests at low to mid-elevations.

Townsend's Solitaire

Townsend's Solitaire

Swainson's Thrush
Catharus ustulatus

The afternoon sun still shines on the ridges while the deep ravines with their rushing waters are already in dark shadow. From the canyon a song begins with a long clear note followed by a series of rich notes spiraling ever higher. The singing continues even as one species after another gradually drops out of the chorus as night approaches. Eventually even the Swainson's Thrush concludes its performance, but the clear lead-in notes continue for a few minutes more. The song of the Swainson's Thrush rivals that of the Hermit Thrush as the most beautiful birdsong in America.

While the Hermit Thrush dwells deep in the conifer forests, the Swainson's prefers the willow and alder thickets that border streams and lakes. The Swainson's Thrush is most often heard in the southern portions of the park. The two species are rather similar in appearance.

The call notes of Swainson's Thrushes are as distinctive as the song and sound like a small pebble dropped into a deep pool. Patience is usually required to observe this brown bird among the shadows of the alders. In time, the singer with the lightly spotted breast may appear seeking insects and other invertebrates on the moist soil along the banks of the stream.

On a late August or September night, the Swainson's Thrush will take off on the beginning of a long journey to their wintering area in southern Mexico. Swainson's Thrushes from the eastern United States have a longer and more difficult journey, traveling to the Amazon Basin after crossing the Gulf of Mexico and the Caribbean.

In addition to invertebrates, they will also eat small seeds and fruits when available. The woven cup nest is concealed close to the ground in dense vegetation. A typical clutch is 4 eggs, and both incubation and the fledgling periods last about 12 days.

Description: The Swainson's Thrush (7") is similar in appearance to the Hermit Thrush but lacks the ruddy tail, and the spots on the breast are not as bold. The brown of the back is warmer in color but the difference is subtle. The face is noticeably tawny. Male and female are similar.

Distribution: Swainson's Thrushes breed in riparian areas across North America from Alaska to the Maritimes in Canada. At Crater Lake, listen for them along Annie Creek or one of the other streams.

Swainson's Thrush

Swainson's Thrush

Hermit Thrush
Catharus guttatus

Deep in the forest understory, in the fading light of a late afternoon, a rich song fills the still air. The song begins with a clear note and then breaks into a jumble of pure bell-like notes. After a pause, the next song begins on a different pitch. The concert will likely continue until the last light, long after the other singers have gone to roost. The singer most often perches 3–20 feet off the ground in a shrub or low in a tree, but is difficult to locate. The song could be coming from almost anywhere, but the singer is often closer than anticipated. Many consider the song of the Hermit Thrush to be the most beautiful in North America. It is related to the Robin but slightly smaller, and it is common among the moister forests but not among the drier pines.

The Hermit Thrush feeds on a variety of invertebrates, often captured by pouncing on to the ground from a low perch. They also use another strategy to find prey—they are foot tremblers. Standing on the ground, they will shift their weight to one foot and tremble the other in the litter. The vibrations are so rapid that they are difficult to see even when very close. Small invertebrates are startled by the vibrations, betray their presence, and are quickly consumed by the thrush. They also readily feed on berries when available, even those of poison oak.

It builds a tidy woven nest near the ground, often in a fern or in a small sapling, where it raises a brood of 4–5 young. Eggs hatch in 12 days and the young fledge in another 12 days.

Description: The reddish-brown tail and speckled breast distinguish the Hermit Thrush (7") from all other birds in the park except the Fox Sparrow. However, the thick bill of the sparrow quickly sets it apart. Also, be careful, because the young of all thrushes (robins, solitaires, and bluebirds) have spotted breasts, if only for a short time. Male and female Hermit Thrushes are similar in appearance.

Distribution: Hermit Thrushes breed in northern coniferous forests throughout much of North America and winter in the southern United States and Mexico in a wide range of habitats. At Crater Lake National Park, Hermit Thrushes are common in the Douglas-fir and true fir forests. In winter they can be found in the snow-free valley bottoms to the west of the Cascades. It is the only spotted thrush to remain in the United States in winter.

Hermit Thrush

Hermit Thrush

American Robin
Turdus migratorius

Some visitors to the park are surprised when an American Robin flies out of a tree to the ground and begins its search for insects and other invertebrates. It seems out of place. This bird is familiar in the back yards in the valleys. Yet, it also breeds high in the Cascades at Crater Lake National Park. They are found almost anywhere there are trees to nest in and ground open enough to exercise their unique style of foraging. They hop or run a few steps along the ground and pause, cocking their head seeking prey. A minor controversy among ornithologists involves whether they are looking for prey or listening for prey. Because both their eyes and ears are located on the sides of their head, it is difficult to know. Current studies show they use both sight and hearing to hunt. Why not?

The Robin is an early riser. Only swallows begin singing earlier, as the first trace of light shows on the eastern horizon. The sweet song is unhurried and is composed of short phrases of clear notes separated by brief pauses. Although song can be heard in almost every month of the year, each male sings most vigorously as a pair starts a new nest. At lower elevations, they may rear two or even three broods in a summer. At higher elevations they typically rear only one. The soft songs heard in the fall and winter are often delivered by young birds sharpening their vocal skills. The 2–4 turquoise eggs are incubated for 12–14 days, and the young fledge in 13 more. Bright blue eggs would seem to invite predation, but it may be that the ability to distinguish brown-spotted cowbird eggs from their own offers greater benefits than penalty. Robins have little need for concern at Crater Lake. Cowbirds seldom venture into the higher elevations.

Description: Both male and female Robins (10") have an orange breast, gray back, and yellow bill. The head of the male is almost black, contrasting with the back. The head of the female is gray. The young are spotted, like all thrushes, but the spots are lost with the late summer molt.

Distribution: American Robins breed broadly across North America. Most populations are migratory, but Robins can be found year-round in Oregon. In winter they can be found just outside the park, among junipers, feeding on the "berries." At Crater Lake National Park they arrive by April and depart by the end of October and are more common along the streams and wetter areas.

American Robin, male

American Robin, female

Evening Grosbeak
Coccothraustes vespertinus

A flock of maybe 40 stubby robin-sized birds flies into the top of a tall fir and disappears. But the sounds continue unabated. The background chatter of burry notes is continuous, punctuated by occasional plaintive calls that carry far in the mountain air. It is fall, and the Evening Grosbeaks are on the move, stripping one more tree of its seeds before moving on. As the flock erupts from the tree, the individuals fly in a tight flock with the undulating path characteristic of its relatives, crossbills and siskins. Evening Grosbeaks breed among the firs of the park and the high country throughout the west. It is, perhaps, the only time of year when you will encounter single birds or pairs.

A closer look reveals the massive pale beak for crushing the largest and hardest of seeds. Hence their name. Their diet is varied. Seeds are a staple, including some of the largest, those of ponderosa and sugar pine. Besides seeds, they feast on spruce budworms during years of population outbreaks as well as other insects. They also are content to feed on the buds of many trees should other energy-rich foods be in short supply. For reasons that are not clear, Evening Grosbeak numbers have declined sharply in recent decades.

Spring migration brings the return of the vocal flocks in the first 2 weeks of May, when they soon disperse into breeding pairs. The nest is a woven cup placed high in a tree, where they typically produce 3–4 eggs. Incubation is performed only by the female. Eggs hatch after a 24-day incubation, and the young fledge in 2 weeks.

Description: The male is unmistakable, with the huge beak and bold yellow line over the eye. The rich brown head grades into a yellow body. When flying, the large white patch in the wings is diagnostic. The female differs markedly, with a gray head and body and a scattering of white markings on the wing instead of a single white patch.

Distribution: Like many of its close relatives, the distribution of the Evening Grosbeak can be unpredictable when not breeding. In winter they descend from the high country and spread across the lowlands as far south as northern Mexico, gathering wherever food is abundant. They breed in the boreal forest across Canada and south through the Rocky Mountains, Cascades, and Sierra Nevada.

Evening Grosbeak, male

Evening Grosbeak, female

Gray-crowned Rosy-Finch
Leucosticte tephrocotis

Maybe you are climbing Garfield Peak or looking out over Crater Lake near the Watchman and happen to see a robust, dark finch scouring the edges of a patch of snow for numbed insects. You are fortunate. This is one of the more difficult birds to find in Oregon. Nowhere are they common and for most of the year they reside only in the mountain air at the tops of the snowcaps in the Cascades and Wallowa Mountain, where snowfields persist into the summer months. To see this bird usually means lacing up the boots, hefting a pack, wearing a generous coat of sunscreen, and taking an ambitious climb for even a chance. Birders from around the state come to Crater Lake for a somewhat less arduous effort to see these birds. Even in winter they are reluctant to abandon the high country for the relative warmth of lower elevations. The closest they may get are the windblown rocky hillsides in the high desert.

Unlike the strategy of many birds, where the male defends an area that encompasses both the nest and the foraging area, the male Rosy-Finch defends the female. Wherever the female goes, the male follows and defends the area immediately around her. Apparently, the female is a more valuable resource than a foraging area in the high country.

By midsummer, Gray-crowned Rosy-Finches gather into flocks. Their black bills have faded to pink and their fall plumage lacks much of the pink seen in the breeding season. At this time they typically frequent the steep hillsides just below the rim. They feed for a short time at one location and then rise almost in unison with noisy chatter, landing a short distance away and begin feeding again.

Rosy-Finches feed on seeds and insects gleaned from the ground and around the margins of snow patches. The woven cup-shaped nest is usually tucked away in a rock crevice, where the bird lays 3–4 eggs. Incubation lasts for 14 days, and the young fledge in another 15–22.

Description: The Gray-crowned Rosy-Finch has a dark brown body (6.25") with a pink rump, belly, and wing coverts. The forehead is black and the face and back of the head are gray. The bill is black when breeding but straw-colored in winter. Females are similar but not as bright.

Distribution: Gray-crowned Rosy-Finches breed high in the mountains from Alaska south to the Sierra Nevada. At Crater Lake they occur in open areas at the highest elevations during the summer months,

Gray-crowned Rosy-Finch, nonbreeding

Gray-crowned Rosy-Finch, breeding

including Vidae Ridge, Dutton Ridge, Garfield Peak, the Watchman, and Llao Rock. They are most often seen on rocky slopes and near the edges of snowfields.

Cassin's Finch
Haemorhous cassinii

A small flock of finches flushes from the ground among the ponderosa pines near the south entrance to the park. The adult males are a bright pink tending to red on the crown, chest, and rump. Females and young males are striped brown and can be very hard to identify. As they fly off, the occasional call of "chiddy-up" is heard. The call is helpful when attempting to identify this species.

There are three species of reddish finches in Oregon, and they can be quite difficult to identify. Both call notes and habitat are helpful when sorting them out. The Purple Finch tends to use a single-note call, unlike the Cassin's Finch. The Purple Finch occurs at lower elevations in the Klamath Basin and in the Douglas-fir forests west of the Cascades. The House Finch occupies more open country and is common around farms and in cities. Fortunately for visitors to the park, identification is easy. Only the Cassin's Finch is common within the park.

In addition to ponderosa pine forests, Cassin's Finches also inhabit the montane forests dominated by true firs. In June and July their song is one of the most frequently heard around the rim. If one is patient, the singer can usually be located high in a fir, one that offers a prominent perch.

The Cassin's Finch feeds on a variety of seeds taken from the ground or trees. The nest is a woven cup placed in a tree, where a clutch of 2–4 eggs is laid. The young hatch in about 12 days and fledge at the age of about 2 weeks.

Description: The male (6.25") has a red head and chest. The belly is white, and the brown wings have two faint wing bars. The male can be distinguished from the male Purple Finch by the bill, which is longer and straighter, and the brown nape (purple in the Purple Finch). The female is lightly striped in brown above and below. It is best told by the longer bill and the lack of a distinct face pattern. Males attain the bright purple plumage in their second year.

Distribution: Cassin's Finches occur in montane coniferous forests from southern Canada to Mexico. At Crater Lake National Park they may be encountered in any open canopied forest, from ponderosa pine to timberline. They are more common at the higher elevations and on the east side of the Cascades. In winter many head for lower elevations, leaving the park.

Cassin's Finch, male

Cassin's Finch, female

Red Crossbill
Loxia curvirostra

The soft "kip-kip-kip" call draws attention to a small flock of birds flying strongly high over the forest. The call and the distinctive undulating flight marks these birds as Red Crossbills.

While all species have their unique stories of adaptation and survival, the Red Crossbill is one of the most peculiar. It is a finch, related to the Cassin's Finch and Pine Siskin. It has a powerful seed eating bill just like other finches, but as the name suggests, the tips of the mandibles cross. The bill is a cone opener. The bird first bites sideways under a cone scale. It then moves its mandible sideways, using the crossed tips as leverage to spread the bracts apart. Once separated, the seeds beneath can be extracted. If the cone resists, the head can be twisted, applying even more leverage to the bract. Experiments have shown that the greater the bill crosses, the more leverage can be applied to a cone. This provides access to an abundant food resource that few others besides squirrels can reach. And, yes, both right- and left-crossed crossbills may be found in the same flock.

There are nine distinct populations of Red Crossbills across North America. The call notes are slightly different for each, some calls are sharp, others are quite soft. Bill size in each population corresponds to the robustness of the principal cones they exploit. In Oregon the bill of the coastal subspecies is relatively small, as they feed largely on the papery cones of the Sitka spruce and the small cones of western hemlock. Those that feed on sturdy ponderosa pinecones at Crater Lake and mountains to the east have larger bills. While the several populations differ in both morphology and behavior, the differences are not large enough in most to warrant their division into separate species. Only the Cassia Crossbill of Idaho has been recently recognized as distinct.

In years when cones are numerous, the crossbills may breed through the winter. They feed largely on the seeds of conifers and even feed their young seeds. They construct a woven nest high in the canopy, and rear about 3 young, which hatch in about 14 days and fledge in 15–25 days. In years when cones are scarce, Crossbills vanish from the park to other areas where cones are plentiful.

Description: The male (6.25") is brick red above and below with brown wings lacking wing bars or other distinctive marks. Young males may

Red Crossbill, male

Red Crossbill, female

show little red. Even adult males vary in color. The female is a uniform dull greenish-yellow. Both have a large distinctive bill and a notched tail. **Distribution:** Red Crossbills breed in coniferous forests across North America. Their abundance tends to vary closely with the size of the cone crop in an area. At Crater Lake National Park they may be exceedingly abundant or rare depending on the availability of food.

Pine Siskin
Spinus pinus

High at the top of a mountain hemlock, a small group of six tiny brown-striped birds hang from the ends of the branches stripping seeds from the cones. There is quiet chatter as they feed. As one cone is exhausted each bird flits to the next. Although there is only a flash of yellow in wing and tail, the Pine Siskin is a goldfinch. It is closely related to its brighter lowland cousins and similar in size.

Siskins are a gregarious species. Except when breeding, they tend to travel in flocks, and flocks may form as early as mid-June. In some years the tops of hemlocks, heavy with tiny cones, may erupt in hundreds of birds flying off in a compact flock in the characteristic undulating flight. In other years you may be lucky to hear an occasional lone bird flying high over the forest. Some forest somewhere distant is laden with cones and filled with noisy birds hanging from the branches. It is difficult to predict when and where they will be abundant either during the breeding season or in winter. They have a variety of calls, but the raspy trill rising in pitch is most distinctive.

Siskins feed on buds and flowers but especially on small seeds taken from cones, and they appear wherever food may be plentiful. At lower elevations to the west of the park, one of their favorite spring foods are the flowers of the Pacific madrone. The nest is a small woven cup usually placed high in a conifer. A typical clutch is 3–4 eggs. Incubation is 13 days, and the young fledge in 13–17 days. If seeds are abundant, the birds may breed quite early in the year. Like other species in the finch family (Fringillidae), they feed their young partially digested seed rather than insects.

Description: The Pine Siskin is a small brown bird (5") striped above and below. The bill is thick at the base and tapers to a sharp point. Individuals vary in the size and brightness of the small yellow patches in the wing and tail. In part, this is associated with sex: males are generally a bit brighter. The tail is notched.

Distribution: Pine Siskins breed in coniferous forests throughout much of North America. In winter they retreat from the more northerly areas in Canada and frequently leave the forests to visit woodlands, farms, and gardens. They are usually one of the most abundant species breeding in the park, found in every forest type. However, they vary in abundance and distribution even within the park boundaries. Few remain in winter.

Pine Siskin

Pine Siskin

Chipping Sparrow

Spizella passerina

Stepping out of the car at a pullout, you might see a small group of tiny brown birds flying to cover. As they fly, they show no distinctive markings. The Chipping Sparrow is one of the least appreciated birds that breeds in Crater Lake National Park. It is easily overlooked. Unless observed at close range, the rusty red cap and bright white line above the eye are difficult to see. Even the song is an insect-like trill that is unlikely to draw your attention.

The Chipping Sparrow has a split distribution within the park. Its song may be heard among the ponderosa pines in the eastern and southern portions of the park, where it forages among the sparse grasses and lupine. The song can also be heard at timberline near the rim and on Mount Scott as it feeds among the knotweed and other plants on the drier pumice soils.

Chipping Sparrows are a favored host of Brown-headed Cowbirds. Eggs deposited in the nest of a Chipping Sparrow by a cowbird hatch a day or two before the eggs of their host, allowing the cowbird young to gain a head start on their nestmates. The larger young cowbird secures most of the food brought by the parents, and the host's young may starve. Chipping Sparrows at lower elevations in the ponderosa pines must contend with this threat, while birds nesting near the rim are safe. Cowbirds are confined to lower elevations.

Chipping Sparrows forage for seeds on the ground much of the year, but during the breeding season also forage for insects on the ground and low in trees. They construct a small neatly woven cup placed low in a tree or shrub. The 3–5 eggs are white speckled with brown. Incubation is 10–12 days and the young fledge in a similar amount of time.

Description: A small (5.5") sparrow with a rufous cap and white line above the eye. The belly is white. It has two fine white wing bars but no white in the tail. Male and female are similar. In fall and winter, they lose the distinctive bright colors and markings on the head.

Distribution: Chipping Sparrows breed in a wide range of habitats across North America and winter in the southern United States and northern Mexico. In Crater Lake National Park they inhabit open parkland at lower elevations and the forest edges near timberline. They arrive

Chipping Sparrow

Chipping Sparrow

at the lower elevations in April, later at higher elevations, and depart by late September.

Fox Sparrow
Passerella iliaca

The Fox Sparrow along with the Green-tailed Towhee are the two shrubland sparrows in the park. The Fox Sparrow is not as brightly colored as the Towhee, being colored in cryptic browns and stripes. However, if there is a pair breeding in the area, it will soon be apparent, as the Fox Sparrow song is both loud and musical. The song, with sharply rising and falling notes, is slightly richer than that of the Green-tailed Towhee, but it takes a trained ear to tell them apart. The loud song ensures its message is carried to neighbors and prospective mates in the dense habitat they occupy.

Despite differences in appearance, the towhee and sparrow are similar in many ways including size, foraging behavior, diet, and choice of habitat. It has been suggested that the similarity in song may help the two species avoid each other, keeping separate territories, thereby minimizing competition between them.

There are several well-defined forms of the Fox Sparrow. The taiga form of the far north is reddish. The coastal form breeding in British Columbia and Alaska is a uniform sooty dark brown on the back. It is the common wintering form at lower elevations in western Oregon. It is the slate-colored form that breeds in the Oregon Cascades including Crater Lake National Park.

The Fox Sparrow is a seedeater for much of the year, the seeds located by scratching among the leaf litter beneath shrubs. During the breeding season it feeds its young a diet composed largely of insects. The cup-shaped nest is concealed on the ground among dense vegetation, where it lays a clutch of 3–4 brown-speckled eggs. Following a 12- to 14-day incubation, the young fledge in another 9–11 days.

Description: The different populations of this widespread bird may one day be recognized as separate species. The debate continues. The form nesting in the park is the "Slate-backed" form. The large brown sparrow (7") has a heavily streaked breast composed of characteristic chevron-shaped spots. The head and back are slate-colored, distinct from the ruddy brown wings and tail. Perhaps the best field mark is the thick bicolored bill; the top of the bill is dark and the bottom pale. Male and female are similar.

Distribution: The Fox Sparrow breeds across Alaska and Canada and south among the mountains of the western United States. They winter

Fox Sparrow, slate-colored form

Fox Sparrow, sooty form

in the valley low to the west and through the southern United States. At Crater Lake, the Fox Sparrow breeds among shrubland near the southern and eastern boundaries of the park. The best chance to observe this bird is to follow its song.

Dark-eyed Junco
Junco hyemalis

Driving along the roads of Crater Lake National Park or hiking along its trails, you will undoubtedly see one or more small birds with dark heads and pink bills flush from your path. The white outer tail feathers flash brightly as they head for cover.

If you pause along one of the trails in the park or at the rim for any length of time, one or more Dark-eyed Junco is likely to reveal itself. They are relatively tame and fearless. As they quietly forage for seeds and small insects on the ground, the white tail feathers show briefly with each hop. The display helps mates silently stay in contact in the breeding season and helps flocks remain together at other times in the year. Occasionally they will give a distinctive sharp call note, especially when disturbed. Dark-eyed Juncos are one of the last to leave when the winter snows arrive in earnest and one of the first to return in spring though the snow is still deep.

Although it is called a junco, it is a sparrow, and it is the only sparrow in Oregon to live deep in the shadows under a forest canopy. Their song is a rich trill, usually on a single pitch, and the songs of different males are different enough in pitch or pace to sometimes be distinguished by human ears.

The adults lack the stripes usually associated with sparrows, but there is no doubt about the immature birds. They are striped. They lose these stripes quickly in the summer molt as they adopt adult plumage when just a couple of months in age.

For much of the year Dark-eyed Juncos glean seeds from the ground. During the breeding season, like many seed eating birds, they also harvest insects. Few birds living at high elevations in the park rear more than a single brood, but the Dark-eyed Junco typically breeds twice or even three times. The nest is a neat woven cup hidden under a log or vegetation. The 3–5 white eggs are speckled brown and hatch in about 12–13 days. The young fledge after only 11 days.

Description: A medium-sized sparrow (6.25"), the adult birds have a black (male) or dark gray (female) hood and a conical pink bill. The sides of the birds nesting in the park are washed in pinkish-brown, and the belly is white. The sides of the dark tail are white.

Distribution: Dark-eyed Juncos are found throughout much of Canada and the United States and display much geographic variation. The

Dark-eyed Junco, male

Dark-eyed Junco, female

Dark-eyed Junco is one of the most abundant birds in the park. It lives in all forest types from lodgepole pine to subalpine fir and Douglas-fir to ponderosa pine. It also occurs both along streams and in the dry meadows.

White-crowned Sparrow
Zonotrichia leucophrys

As a breeding bird, White-crowned Sparrows are a relatively new addition to the park. Listen for the clear song among the willows and mountain ash thickets near the mountain meadows. It is a complex song, beginning with a long pure tone followed by a combination of pure tones, trills, and vibrato notes. The song sounds melancholy to many. Different populations have distinct dialects including more than one in Oregon. Dialects are learned from their father or more often other nearby males, either as dependent young after fledging or soon after independence. Once the song is heard during this brief time, a young male will sing a near perfect copy of this specific song as it establishes its first territory the following spring. If for some reason it does not hear a White-crowned Sparrow song during this sensitive time shortly after fledging, it will never be able to sing a proper White-crowned Sparrow song.

Individual dialects are known to persist for several decades, and as we continue to study these birds, we are likely to learn they endure a century or more. A single song heard as birds tune up for spring on the wintering area can reveal where the bird will be in a few weeks' time, courting a female and hoping to start a family. Unlike many birds, the female also sings occasionally.

The White-crowned Sparrow is a common migrant both in May and again in late August and September, staying close to brushy cover and at forest edges where the foliage is close to the ground. At these times White-crowned Sparrows travel in flocks and may be joined by their close relative the Golden-crowned Sparrow. While the appearance of adult White-crowned Sparrows is distinctive, a majority of the fall migrants are nondescript immature birds with poorly defined chestnut stripes on the head and a pink bill.

White-crowned Sparrows are ground foragers in and around brush patches, where they feed mostly on seeds. They construct a woven cup placed low in a shrub or on the ground. The 3–5 lightly speckled eggs hatch in 12 days, and the young fledge 8–10 days later.

Description: A moderately large sparrow (9.5") and distinctively marked. Male and female are similar in having a pink bill and a black-and-white striped crown. The back is brown and the belly gray. Their wings have two wing bars. Immature birds lack the distinctive black-and-white crown.

White-crowned Sparrow, adult

White-crowned Sparrow, immature

Distribution: The White-crowned Sparrow is widespread in Canada and western North America, breeding in open areas with light brush. They occur from timberline to the coast. Small numbers breed in the park but are abundant spring and fall migrants. The easiest place to find breeding birds is at Munson Meadows near the headquarters. The brushy areas near timberline and in the area of the Pinnacles are good places to find small flocks of migrating birds.

Lincoln's Sparrow
Melospiza lincolnii

There are many more-brightly colored birds in the park. There are many that capture your attention because they are large, display unusual behavior, or simply are more visible. The Lincoln's Sparrow fails on each point. Yet they are an integral part of the diverse collection of species that makes up the interconnected community of life at Crater Lake National Park.

This small but neatly marked sparrow favors the willow and alder thickets at the headwaters of streams in the high country throughout Oregon, but nowhere are they abundant. They are content to move quietly among the thick tangle of vegetation as they forage. Even when they rise from the shadows to sing, they often choose a concealed perch. The enthusiastic song is a bright flurry of fluid notes that lacks a pattern. The song is part of the background of the spring chorus, singled out for appreciation only if you happen to be very close to the singer.

It takes patience to see this secretive bird among the tangle of willows. The first glimpse may be of a dark, almost black, bird as it darts across an opening. If you remain still, it may return to its search for seeds or gleaning insects from the moist ground at the water's edge. It is a close relative of the familiar Song Sparrow that breeds along streams and in back yards at lower elevations, and it takes a careful observer to distinguish between the two.

Lincoln's Sparrows usually feed both on the ground and among the vegetation of dense shrubs. The woven cup-shaped nest is typically concealed on the ground, where they lay 4–5 brown-speckled eggs. Incubation lasts 11–13 days and the young fledge in 10–11 days.

Description: A small, dark, striped, brown sparrow (5.75"). There is no white in the wing or tail. The Lincoln's Sparrow is smaller than the Song Sparrow with finer striping, gray face, and buffy "moustache." Male and female are similar.

Distribution: Lincoln's Sparrows breed in Alaska, Canada, and the mountain west. Most migrate to the southern United States and Mexico in winter, but some remain in weedy fields at lower elevations in the Pacific Northwest. During the breeding season they are found near wet mountain meadows. At Crater Lake National Park, they can be found in Munson Meadows near the park headquarters.

Lincoln's Sparrow

Lincoln's Sparrow

Green-tailed Towhee
Pipilo chlorurus

Towhees are the largest sparrows in North America. Six species occur in the United States, but only the Green-tailed Towhee is found in the high country. The name "towhee" comes from the call of a different species and has been attached to this and several other large sparrows. Only the Fox Sparrow rivals them in size, and it lives alongside the Green-tailed Towhee in the shrubland of the park. Both favor the leaf litter under a dense cover of ceanothus (often called snowbrush), manzanita, and bitterbrush. When they sing, each tends to sing from an exposed perch well above the brush, providing the best opportunity to see one. Both sing loud fluid songs that can be frustratingly similar. In good light the green in the wings and tail of the Green-tailed Towhee almost glows. With singing over, it drops to the ground among dense cover to feed. It scratches among the leaf litter for seeds and insects.

Fires thin out the trees in the ponderosa pine zone and promote shrub growth in drier habitats. This favors towhees a decade or so after a fire. As the trees fill in, the shrubs thin out and the towhees leave, seeking out younger more vigorous shrubland.

Recurring fires that remove vegetation and even entire swaths of forests are part of the normal cycle of life in southern Oregon forests, especially among lodgepole and ponderosa pines. The orderly sequence of vegetation that returns between fires is called "biological succession." Animals, too, participate in this progression, including the Green-tailed Towhee. Each species arrives and thrives for the duration their preferred habitat is available. As the habitat changes, the current set of inhabitants yields to the next. All are dependent on regular fires in nearby areas to reset the environment to earlier stages in succession and create new habitat.

Most of the year Green-tailed Towhees feed on seeds, but like most sparrows, it adds insects to the diet during the breeding season. The cup-shaped nest is concealed on the ground among dense vegetation. The 4 brown-speckled eggs hatch in about 12 days, and the young spend 11–14 days in the nest before fledging.

Description: The Green-tailed Towhee is a striking bird slightly smaller than a robin (7.25") with a rufous cap and white throat. The back, wings, and tail are a bright olive green. The belly is largely gray. Male and female are similar.

Green-tailed Towhee

Green-tailed Towhee

Distribution: Green-tailed Towhees breed throughout the mountain shrubland of the western United States. Most winter in Mexico. At Crater Lake they inhabit the dense shrubs in the ponderosa pine parkland in the southeast portion of the park. After breeding they may also be found at higher elevations about the rim.

Nashville Warbler

Leiothlypis ruficapilla

The shrubland near Sun and Annie Creeks comes alive with song in May with the return of the Nashville Warbler, but the source of the song rarely emerges for a clear view. Follow the song and with patience you might be lucky enough to see this small bird with the bright yellow belly and gray face and crown. Listen closely to the songs. Each male sings one song, but the several males in a population sing a variety of songs. The differences are great enough that, with a little care, one can often distinguish among many individuals. The season of song is brief among Nashville Warblers. They are one of the first birds to cease singing as spring transitions to summer, often falling silent as early as the second half of June.

This is the only warbler in Oregon that regularly nests on the ground. As soon as the young fledge in late June and early July, they, like so many other summer birds breeding in the park, follow spring up the mountain. The Nashville Warbler feeds close to the ground and is often seen in the brush around the rim and along the path down to the boat landing in Cleetwood Cove in August and early September.

Nashville Warblers feed on insects gleaned from shrubs and seedlings. They construct a cup-shaped nest hidden among dense vegetation. The 4–5 brown-speckled eggs hatch after an 11- to 12-day incubation, and the young fledge 11–12 days later.

Description: The Nashville Warbler (4.75") is a small greenish-yellow bird with a bright yellow belly and throat. The top and sides of the head are gray, and if viewed from above the tiny red crown patch may be seen. The white eye ring is distinctive. Male and female are similar in appearance.

Distribution: There are two breeding populations, one in eastern North America and one in the west. Some suggest the two represent different species. The western population breeds from southern British Columbia south through the Cascades and Sierra Nevada to southern California. They winter in the lowlands of Mexico and Central America. In the park, Nashville Warblers are most common in the brushy areas especially among the ceanothus growing beneath the ponderosa pine near the southern entrance. They also inhabit the riparian areas along the creeks. They arrive by early May and depart by mid-September.

Nashville Warbler

Nashville Warbler

MacGillivray's Warbler

Geothlypis tolmiei

This shy but vocal warbler lives in the willows and alders along Sun and Annie Creeks. It also lives in similar habitat around some of the moist mountain meadows such as Munson Meadow near the park headquarters. It is never far from water, or at least moist habitat, when breeding. When foraging in dense cover close to the ground, the loud call note might be the only clue that the bird is about. However, when it sings, it climbs out of the tangle of leaves to an exposed perch 10–30 feet above the ground. This is the best chance for seeing this striking bird. The two-part song is fluid but slightly burry and sounds to some like "sweeter-sweeter-sweeter-sugar-sugar," the second phrase somewhat lower in pitch. During the fall migration take care to distinguish it from Orange-crowned, Wilson's, and Yellow Warblers that pause in the riparian areas to feed a while before moving on. All are greenish-yellow with few distinctive features at this time of year.

During the Pleistocene, ice sheets advanced and retreated several times. At the greatest extent, the glaciers divided the boreal forest of North America into eastern and western portions. During these periods of isolation, a number of birds evolved into distinct species that were no longer able to interbreed when the ice sheets retreated, and the boreal forest became one again. We see the evidence of this pattern with species like Eastern and Western Wood-Pewees, Lazuli and Indigo Buntings, Black-headed and Rose-breasted Grosbeaks, Black-throated Green and Townsend's Warblers, Western and Scarlet Tanagers, and Mourning and MacGillivray's Warblers.

Mourning and MacGillivray's Warblers are similar in appearance, with small differences in markings about the eye and throat as well as song. They do not interbreed. Their current ranges meet in a narrow zone in northern Alberta.

The MacGillivray's Warbler feeds on insects gleaned from low vegetation and rears 3–5 young in a cup-shaped nest placed in a shrub, sometimes on the ground. The brown-speckled eggs hatch in 11–13 days and the young fledge in 8–9 days.

Description: The male (5.25") has a bright yellow belly with a greenish back. The entire head is gray with a thin bill. The hood grades to black where it abruptly meets the yellow belly. Small white marks above and

MacGillivray's Warbler, male

MacGillivray's Warbler, female

below the eye are distinctive. The wing and tail are greenish-yellow. The female is similar, but the hood is paler.

Distribution: MacGillivray's Warbler breeds in riparian areas in the western United States and Canada and winters in Mexico and northern Central America. In the park it inhabits streamside vegetation and the borders of mountain meadows from May into September.

Yellow-rumped Warbler

Setophaga coronata

On Wizard Island a small bird darts out of a mountain hemlock to capture a flying insect. Large white patches in the wing and corners of the tail flash brightly in the mountain sun. A soft but assertive call note is often heard as it forages. The Yellow-rumped Warbler is a foliage gleaner like most warblers, but it also catches insects like a flycatcher. Dislodging an insect from a branch, it may tumble after its prey until snatching it up, often before it lands on the ground.

This warbler occurs in every forest type in the park, from riparian vegetation to white firs to lodgepole pines. It is one of the few birds that can be considered common among the lodgepole pines. The Yellow-rumped Warbler is the first warbler to arrive in spring (mid-April) and the last to leave (October). In late July and early August, the male loses its bright colors as it molts in preparation for the upcoming migration.

The song of the Yellow-rumped Warbler is difficult to describe. It is slower-paced than the songs of many warblers and has a cheerful feel. The short song has two parts, with the second part typically higher in pitch, but sometimes this is reversed. The syllables that compose each phrase contain two or three notes and are more complex than those of many other warblers.

Yellow-rumped Warblers feed largely on insects taken from foliage or from the air in flycatcher fashion. They occasionally feed on sap at sapsucker wells and on fruit. The neat woven cup-shaped nest is hidden among the foliage, and the 4–5 eggs are lightly speckled brown. Incubation is 12–13 days, as is the fledgling period. Yellow-rumped Warblers at lower elevations sometimes rear two broods a year.

Description: The male "Audubon's" form of the Yellow-rumped Warbler (5.5") has a black chest, with yellow on the crown, throat, sides and rump, large white wing bars, and a flash of white in the tail. The female is paler and lacks the black chest. Females still show the yellow marks and the white in the tail.

Distribution: Yellow-rumped Warblers breed across North America in boreal forests. The yellow-throated "Audubon's" form occurs in the west. In southern Oregon it achieves its highest densities in white fir forests. It is common in the park and may be encountered almost everywhere. In winter it does not migrate as far south as most warblers, wintering

Yellow-rumped Warbler, male

Yellow-rumped Warbler, female

across the southern United States. Small numbers even winter at lower elevations in western Oregon.

Hermit Warbler
Setophaga occidentalis

"Hermit" is an appropriate name for this species. Although it is one of the most abundant birds breeding in the coniferous forests of the western portion of the state, it is seldom seen. Considering the bright lemon-yellow head, it is even more surprising. As a breeding bird, the Hermit Warbler is not common in the park. Spring comes too late to the mountain conifers to provide the food necessary to rear young.

Listen for its song in the forest at the lower elevations in the park. Becoming familiar with their hurried songs helps to locate the males as they forage among the highest branches of a very tall canopy.

Unlike many birds, Hermit Warblers sing two very different songs, the functions of which are not entirely clear. The songs differ from area to area, forming dialects. One song is similar among all the males in an area that may cover hundreds of square miles or more and is apparently used, in part, to attract a mate. The dialect sung by males in the Panhandle is common in the Cascades south to the California border but differs markedly from the song sung by the males at the west entrance. This song is sung along the western slopes of the Cascades from Prospect to Willamette Pass. The second song of the males is variable among individuals—each tends to sing a unique song. The second song serves a function in maintaining a territory. However, there appears to be much more to the story, and the use of song continues to be studied.

Hermit Warblers feed on insects gleaned from the foliage of conifers. They construct a cup-shaped nest on a limb, usually protected from above, where they rear 4–5 young. Little is known of the incubation or fledgling period of this retiring bird, but both are likely to be about 12 days in duration. Squirrels are one of the chief predators on warbler nests.

Description: The male (5") has a bright lemon-yellow head. The black eye stands out on the unmarked face. The back of the head and throat are black. The back is gray and belly white. It has two white wing bars, and the sides of the tail are white. The female is similar, but not as brightly colored and shows little of the black throat patch.

Distribution: The Hermit Warbler breeds in the coniferous mountain forests of the Cascades and Sierra Nevada west to the coast and winters in the mountains of Mexico and northern Central America. In the park it breeds at the lower elevations near the west entrance and in the

Hermit Warbler, male

Hermit Warbler, male

Panhandle. It is an irregular and sparse breeder at the higher elevations. Just outside the park, especially to the west, it becomes more abundant. After breeding many move up the mountain beginning in mid-July, where they prepare for the southern migration.

Western Tanager
Piranga ludoviciana

One of the most beautiful birds to breed in Oregon is the Western Tanager. It belongs to a group of birds common in the tropics. Tropical birds, especially tanagers, are often strikingly colored in every shade imaginable. They include vivid reds, penetrating blues, gold, and even emerald green. Still others are a combination of all these. Bright colors are apparently not a bold advertisement among the shadows of dense rainforest foliage, where these birds still manage to avoid the attention of predators. We are fortunate that this refugee from the tropics comes north each year to breed.

Although called a "tanager," recent studies have found the Western Tanager is more closely related to cardinals and buntings and not to the host of "true" tanagers. It makes little difference. The families are closely related.

The Western Tanager is a deliberate forager. While many foliage gleaners in the forests move rapidly through the canopy, barely pausing in their relentless search for insect prey, the tanager takes its time. It scans the foliage for the choicest prey, often a large caterpillar or moth. Once the target is spotted, the bird dashes out a meter or more and plucks the insect from a branch or needle. However, the bill is designed more for eating fruit than insects. It is large and has a small "tooth" on each side that neatly slices the fruits found in the tropics. It gets little use in the breeding season, but at this time it is more important to feed the young a diet high in protein. Western Tanagers are found in every coniferous forest and woodland in the state except for juniper.

The distinctive two-note call will help locate this bird. It is a toneless "pit-tick." The song is a short series of phrases, reminiscent of a Robin's song but slightly quicker and harsher.

The Western Tanager constructs a neat woven cup nest concealed high among the vegetation. It typically lays 3–5 lightly speckled eggs, which hatch in 13 days. The young fledge in 11 days.

Description: The orange head, yellow body, and black wings make the male of this species (7.25") unmistakable. The male also sports two white wing bars. The female is drab, with only a wash of yellow and two white wing bars.

Western Tanager, male

Western Tanager, female

Distribution: The Western Tanager breeds from northern Canada to the Mexican border in Western North America and winters in Mexico and Central America. From May through August it is widespread in the park in most forest types. A few remain into September. After breeding, some follow spring up the mountain and visit the highest forests. Perhaps the easiest place to see tanagers in the park is among the open ponderosa and lodgepole pines.

Lazuli Bunting
Passerina amoena

At the top of a willow along Annie Creek, a small turquoise blue bird with an orange breast and finch-like bill sings loudly. The bright song, without a clear pattern, includes numerous doubled notes. Just as you focus in on the singer, it dives into the dense vegetation. For such a brightly colored bird, it is difficult to view.

The bird seems out of place. It seems too brightly colored to be native to the Pacific Northwest among less colorful sparrows and fly-catchers. Colors like these are seen only in cages or in tropical forests, or so it seems. However, it is a native. The genus *Passerina* consists of seven species of brightly colored buntings, and most are found in more tropical habitats in the southern United States and Central America. The brightest of all is the Painted Bunting, whose range extends north into Florida and Texas.

The Lazuli Bunting, like the Indigo Bunting of the eastern United States, returns to the tropics each winter. They are neotropical migrants and seem eager to retreat to their subtropical wintering grounds in Mexico soon after fledging their young in late June and early July. Few are seen after mid-August. However, take care, the males lose much of their bright plumage with the midsummer molt. The Lazuli Bunting favors brushy areas, especially along creeks. In other areas it frequents oak woodlands and hedgerows.

The Lazuli Bunting is a seedeater much of the year, but in the breeding season feeds extensively on insects gleaned from the foliage. It weaves a tidy cup-shaped nest in a shrub or low in a tree, where it lays 3–4 eggs. Incubation lasts 12 days, and the young fledge in another 9–11. Both parents care for the young.

Description: The male (5.5") has a turquoise head and back and a short finch-like bill. The breast is orange and belly is white. The wing has a single white wing bar that, along with its thick bill, helps distinguish it from the bluebirds. The female is drab, with only the slightest hint of blue in the wing and on the rump and orange on the breast.

Distribution: The breeding range of the Lazuli Bunting is largely con-fined to the western United States. In the park they inhabit the meadows and stream sides wherever willows and alder are found, from the rim to the lowest elevations along Annie Creek between May and August.

Lazuli Bunting, male

Lazuli Bunting, female

Munson Meadows, Annie Creek, and Wheeler Creek at the Pinnacles offer good chances to see these birds.

Some Places to Bird in Crater Lake National Park and Beyond

Because of the great variation in habitats, you are likely to encounter new species during any stop or walk in the park. While fascinating birds can be found at any location, the following areas are of particular interest.

The Watchman and Mount Scott

Time at the higher points in the park is well spent, especially in late August and September. Birding can be productive from the rim at the parking area to the Watchman and along the trail up to the lookout. The trail to the summit of Mount Scott may also produce good results. Two of the most sought-after birds in the park can often be found here. The Rock Wren is hard to miss if it is active. Wait for their ringing call and search the rocky slopes for the small bird basking in the mountain sun from the top of some boulder.

The Gray-crowned Rosy-Finch is more challenging to find. It is common at times but scarce or absent at others. Be patient and scan the slopes inside the crater for flocks of finch-like birds. Their occasional busy chatter will often help locate a foraging flock among the talus. Check out the areas around melting patches of snow, as they often feed on numbed insects trapped there. Rosy-Finches are "nervous" feeders and frequently relocate. They fly in tight groups with characteristic undulating flight.

The rim is a corridor for migrants including Cooper's Hawks, Sharp-shinned Hawks, Red-tailed Hawks, Northern Harriers, Peregrine Falcons, Prairie Falcons, and Vaux's Swifts. Other birds about the rim include American Pipits, Mountain Bluebirds, Mountain Chickadees, Red-breasted Nuthatches, Yellow-rumped Warblers, Dark-eyed Juncos, White-crowned Sparrows, Pine Siskins, and Cassin's Finches. Clark's Nutcrackers and Canada Jays are fixtures.

Crater Lake

The lake itself provides modest birding. California Gulls are the most common birds on the lake and can usually be observed on any summer or fall day. Small flocks of Common Mergansers may be seen foraging in the shallows. Spotted Sandpipers and American Dippers forage along the shoreline, and Violet-green Swallows fly overhead. In recent years a pair of breeding Bald Eagles has been present and can often be observed from the boat earlier in the season. Late in the season, including the latter part of September and all of October, be on the watch for a variety of ducks, grebes, phalaropes, and other migrants pausing on the lake before moving on. Given the general lack of food, they seldom stay long.

Annie Creek and the Panhandle

Some of the best birding in the park is along Annie Creek in and near the Panhandle at the southern entrance. Lower elevations mean an earlier green-up and more birds in both species and number. The chorus of breeding birds along the creek in June and July should yield most of the common species including Western Flycatchers, Swainson's Thrushes, Lazuli Buntings, Wilson's Warblers, and MacGillivray's Warblers.

In the white firs outside the canyon, listen for Pileated Woodpeckers, Cassin's Vireos, Mountain Chickadees, Hermit Warblers, and Western Tanagers. Areas with ponderosa pine and shrubland beneath harbor White-headed Woodpeckers, Nashville Warblers, and sometimes Green-tailed Towhees and Fox Sparrows.

Munson Meadows

The wet meadows and surrounding forest around the headquarters is one of the most productive areas for birds above 6000'. Some of the species breeding among the willows include Lazuli Buntings, MacGillivray's Warblers, White-crowned Sparrows, and Lincoln's Sparrows. Away from the wet meadows in the surrounding forest look for Hairy Woodpeckers, Steller's Jays, Canada Jays, Hermit Thrushes, Golden-crowned Kinglets, and Dark-eyed Juncos. In late summer other species join them from lower elevations or farther north including Cassin's Vireos, Black-headed Grosbeaks, Orange-crowned Warblers, Black-throated Gray Warblers, Hermit Warblers, and Townsend's Warblers.

Mazama Village

Mazama Village, including the campground, is located among lodgepole pines with a young understory of true fir. Common birds here are Canada Jays, Steller's Jays, Red-breasted Nuthatches, Brown Creepers, Golden-crowned Kinglets, Ruby-crowned Kinglets, Hermit Thrushes, Yellow-rumped Warblers, and Dark-eyed Juncos. In late summer and fall other species may visit including Varied Thrushes, Black-headed Grosbeaks, Orange-crowned Warblers, and Townsend's Warblers. The trail into the canyon from the campground will take you into wet meadows and other open areas along Annie Creek. There you might find Rufous Hummingbirds, Dipper, and maybe even a Belted Kingfisher.

Boundary Springs

Lodgepole pines are not the most productive of habitats for birds, but the trail to the springs is one of the best places to find a lodgepole pine specialist, the Black-backed Woodpecker. Be patient and listen for the soft calls. Other summer residents include Red-breasted Nuthatches, Brown Creepers, a few Western Tanagers, Yellow-rumped Warblers, Dark-eyed Juncos, and Red Crossbills. Pacific Wrens and American Robins can be found along the creeks. Turkey Vultures, which tend to avoid the highest elevations in the park, may be seen here.

Cleetwood Trail to the Boat Landing

The patches of green-leaf manzanita along the trail to the boat dock are a great place to find migrant birds in late summer. Listen for their call notes among the brush to locate them, as they are largely silent after leaving their breeding territories. Regularly seen species here include Orange-crowned Warblers, Wilson's Warblers, MacGillivray's Warblers, White-crowned Sparrows, and Green-tailed Towhees. Other birds you are likely to see and hear include Red-breasted Nuthatches, Mountain Chickadees, Dark-eyed Juncos, Townsend's Solitaires, and Clark's Nutcrackers.

Pinnacle Valley

The road to the Pinnacles begins with alder-filled wet meadows, continues down the slope through lodgepole pine, and ends in more lodgepole pine with a bitterbrush understory. Closer to the rim, Lazuli Buntings and Western Tanagers are sometimes common. Also listen for Golden-crowned Kinglets, Cassin's Finches, Hairy Woodpeckers, Red-breasted Nuthatches, Brown Creepers, Mountain Chickadees, and Dark-eyed Juncos. Among the lodgepole pines a careful visitor may find both Black-backed and American Three-toed Woodpeckers. At the Pinnacles Overlook, Violet-green Swallows are reliable. In some years you may hear Fox Sparrows or Green-tailed Towhees.

Pumice Desert

The large open expanses of the Pumice Desert and similar areas to the north of the rim are not especially productive areas for birds. The sparse cover of knotweed and other plants produce a crop of seeds attracting a variety of sparrows and other birds in migration including Chipping Sparrows, White-crowned Sparrows, and American Pipits. Most of the activity occurs around the margins of the openings where Mountain Bluebirds, Cassin's Finches, Chipping Sparrows, Dark-eyed Juncos and Yellow-rumped Warblers are the most common species. In the late summer and fall, post-breeding and migrant hawks are common. Watch for Red-tailed Hawks, Cooper's Hawks, Sharp-shinned Hawks, Northern

Pumice Desert

Harriers, Prairie Falcons, and the occasional Golden Eagle. Most of the Red-tailed Hawks will be immature birds lacking the orange tails of adults.

Red Blanket Creek

Not often seen by visitors, Red Blanket Creek grazes the southwest corner of the park. The trail into the Sky Lakes Wilderness includes the lowest elevations in Crater Lake National Park west of the crest of the Cascades. The trail up Red Blanket Creek meets the Pacific Crest Trail leading north into the park. Beginning at the trailhead outside of Prospect, Douglas-fir and western hemlock are common, quickly giving way to white fir at higher elevations. A fire passed through the area in 2008, consuming the understory, but left the old-growth canopy largely intact. Common birds include Hermit Warblers, Chestnut-backed Chickadees, Dark-eyed Juncos, Hairy Woodpeckers, Red-breasted Sapsuckers, Golden-crowned Kinglets, Red-breasted Nuthatches, and Brown Creepers. This is the only place I have encountered Mountain Quail in the park.

BIRDS BEYOND CRATER LAKE NATIONAL PARK

While Crater Lake National Park supports a rather select group of birds, the surrounding area is renowned for its diversity. In this section, descriptions of the habitat and birds most often encountered in these areas are included, with a focus on other National Park Service units.

Oregon Caves National Monument

Oregon Caves National Monument is located about 90 miles to the southwest of Crater Lake National Park. To reach the monument, travel to the town of Cave Junction and turn east at the south end of town. You first drive through a mix of agricultural land, woodlots, riparian area, and oak woodland. Watch for Acorn Woodpeckers, Anna's Hummingbirds, Ash-throated Flycatchers, Western Wood-Pewees, Western Bluebirds, Bewick's Wrens, California Towhees, and Lesser Goldfinches. Along the streams be alert for Red-shouldered Hawks, Black Phoebes, Western Warbling Vireos, Yellow-breasted Chats, and Lazuli Buntings.

Soon the road enters the mixed conifer-hardwood forest. The forest is dense and diverse, with a mix of older and younger stands; the oldest are more than 200 years old. The variety is due to both a long history of fire in this region, to which the forest is well-adapted, and to timber harvest outside the boundaries of the monument. The forest is dominated by Douglas-fir, with lesser numbers of sugar and ponderosa pine vying for their spot of sun among the canopy. Beneath the canopy, Pacific madrone (*Arbutus menziesii*), California black oak (*Quercus kelloggii*), tanoak (*Lithocarpus* sp.), and incense cedar (*Calocedrus decurrens*) are common. Watch for Port Orford cedar (*Chamaecyparis lawsoniana*) and knobcone pine (*Pinus attenuata*) along the way. The small evergreen tree with small leaves, many looking like miniature holly leaves, is the canyon live oak (*Quercus chrysolepis*), a favorite of birds. Oregon Caves, though it is high in the Siskiyou Mountains, lies at a lower elevation than Crater Lake National Park. The growing season is longer here, and a higher diversity of plants thrive.

The greater productivity contributes to greater bird diversity. The forest resounds in song from April through June, but it is often a challenge to locate the inhabitants among the forest canopy. Though the two park units share many species, several are found only at Oregon Caves. The Hutton's Vireos and Black-throated Gray Warblers (*right*) favor canyon live oak but may be found in other habitats as well. Chestnut-backed

Chickadees and Hermit Warblers are common. Other birds frequently heard and seen in the area include Mountain Quail, Vaux's Swifts, Rufous Hummingbirds, Red-breasted Sapsuckers, Pileated Woodpeckers, Northern Flickers, Western Flycatchers, Cassin's Vireos, Steller's Jays, Common Ravens, Red-breasted Nuthatches, Brown Creepers, Hermit Thrushes, Golden-crowned Kinglets, Townsend's Solitaires, Black-headed Grosbeaks (*below*), MacGillivray's Warblers, Orange-crowned Warblers, Nashville Warblers, Western Tanagers, Spotted Towhees, Dark-eyed Juncos, Purple Finches, and Pine Siskins.

The buzzy song of the Black-throated Gray Warbler fills the live oak slopes beginning in early April.

Brightly colored Black-headed Grosbeaks are easily located by their loud and fluid song.

Lava Beds National Monument

South of the lakes in the Klamath Basin on the northern flanks of Medicine Hat is another unit of the National Park System. Lava Beds National Monument lies at the interface between the forests of the Cascades and the shrub-steppe of the high desert. From the headquarters, which sits among western juniper and sage in addition to a diverse shrubland, the land falls away north to the marshes, offering a spectacular vista of changing vegetation.

The masked Loggerhead Shrike frequently perches on power lines and other exposed perches seeking insect and small vertebrate prey.

Black-billed Magpies are widespread and inquisitive.

Among the junipers, sagebrush (*Artemisia tridentata*), and choke-cherries (*Prunus virginianus*) around the headquarters, watch for Oak Tit-mice, Bewick's Wrens, California Towhees, Chipping Sparrows, Common Nighthawks, Townsend's Solitaires, California Quail, Northern Flickers, Green-tailed Towhees, Loggerhead Shrikes (*left*), Mountain Bluebirds, and Mountain Chickadees. A fortunate visitor may even see Purple Mar-tin. A small colony nests in one of the caves on the monument.

In the Petroglyph Unit of the monument, located just to the east of Tulelake, the cliffs are inhabited by a variety of birds not found elsewhere in the national monument. Watch for American Kestrels, Golden Eagles, Prairie Falcons, and Red-tailed Hawks flying along the rim. American Barn Owls and Great Horned Owls roost in the sheltered recesses of the cliff face. White-throated Swifts, Rock Pigeons, Say's Phoebes, Western Kingbirds, Black-billed Magpies (*left*), Common Ravens, Rock Wrens, and Canyon Wrens all nest here. Cliff Swallows, with their gourd-shaped mud nests, are abundant. Clouds of Cliff Swallows will pour from the cliffs if a bird of prey approaches too closely. Brewer's Blackbirds, West-ern Meadowlarks, House Finches, Mourning Doves, and the occasional Sage Thrasher and Loggerhead Shrike may be found in the shrubs around the foot of the cliffs.

Cascade-Siskiyou National Monument

The Cascade-Siskiyou National Monument, managed by the Bureau of Land Management, was established in 2000 to protect the incredible diversity of plant and animal life found here. The monument is located in the hills a few miles to the southeast of Ashland. The monument straddles the junction between the Cascade Mountains, oriented north and south on the east, and the Siskiyou Mountains, oriented east and west to the west. The two meet where Interstate-5 crosses from Oregon to California.

Within the monument you can find plants characteristic of the moun-tains in the Great Basin growing alongside plants from the Coast Ranges, the High Cascades, and the Central Valley of California. Birch leaf and curl-leaf mountain mahogany (*Cercocarpus betuloides, C. ledifolius*) grow side by side, as well as Oregon white oak (*Quercus garryana*) and big sage.

The birds, too, reflect this diversity. Green-tailed Towhees and Brewer's Sparrows from the arid regions to the east nest alongside Acorn Woodpeckers, Oak Titmice, and Anna's Hummingbirds from the west.

The monument also harbors one of the largest populations of Great Gray Owls (*below*) in the continental United States.

Other birds common on the monument include Hermit Warblers, Pileated Woodpeckers, Red-breasted Sapsuckers, Mountain Bluebirds, Vesper Sparrows, Sandhill Cranes (*below*), Williamson's Sapsuckers, Cassin's Vireos, Golden-crowned Kinglets, Dark-eyed Juncos, Cassin's Finches, Yellow-rumped Warblers, Steller's Jays, Canada Jays, White-headed Woodpeckers, Townsend's Solitaires, and Sooty Grouse.

The best opportunity to locate the secretive Great Gray Owl is at the margins of the mountain meadows at dusk.

Sandhill Cranes occur as widely scattered pairs in meadows near the mountain lakes.

Klamath Basin National and State Wildlife Refuges

In stark contrast to the select group of birds at Crater Lake National Park, the lake basin just to the south teems with species of all kinds. The wildlife refuges of the Klamath Basin, along with Malheur National Wildlife Refuge to the east, have been named among the ten best birding places in the United States. In May it is possible to observe more than 120 species in a day's outing on the Lower Klamath Lake and Tulelake National Wildlife Refuges. Diverse waterfowl abound at all seasons. One of the favorites is the Cinnamon Teal (*below*). Late March and April and again in October and November are the best times to see migrating geese. Late April and early May are the best times to find large numbers of migrating shorebirds. The latter half of May presents the best of the breeding birds including Eared Grebes, both Western and Clark's Grebes, White Pelicans, White-faced Ibis, Black-crowned Night Herons, Willets, Wilson's Phalaropes, Black-necked Stilts, American Avocets, Franklin's Gulls, Black Terns, Forster's Terns (*next page*), Marsh Wrens, Yellow-headed Blackbirds, and Tricolored Blackbirds, in addition to the waterfowl. Listen for American Bitterns, Sora, and Virginia Rails hidden among the rushes. A determined birder may find a Long-billed Curlew or Sandhill Crane. The only time you may wish to avoid the refuges of

The male Cinnamon Teal is one of the most brightly colored ducks in the marsh in spring.

Forster's Terns fly slowly over the marsh in search of small fish and other aquatic prey.

the Klamath Basin is during June and July, when the mosquitoes reign supreme. Even the depths of winter produce abundant waterfowl and raptors, especially Bald Eagles and Tundra Swans. This is also a time when you may be lucky enough to discover Lapland Longspurs or even wintering Gray-crowned Rosy-Finches.

You may wish to attend the Winter Wings Festival in February or the Migratory Bird Festival in May. Contact the Klamath Falls Chamber of Commerce or the Headquarters of the Klamath Basin National Wildlife Refuges for details.

ROGUE VALLEY

The winter chill of the high country of Crater Lake National Park is matched by the summer heat in the valleys to the west. The Rogue Valley lies at the northern end of the California Floristic Province, and its unique flora and fauna are defined by its Mediterranean climate. Several bird species reach the northern limit of their distribution along with the chaparral and other communities from California.

The best place to see many of these species is at Upper and Lower Table Rock, just north of Medford. The Nature Conservancy and the Bureau of Land Management maintain trails at these locations and conduct guided walks in the spring. During the breeding season you can find Wild Turkey, Mourning Doves, Anna's Hummingbirds, Acorn Wood-peckers, Western Wood-Pewees, Ash-throated Flycatchers (*below*), Violet-green Swallows, California Scrub-Jays, Western Bluebirds, Blue-gray Gnatcatchers, Oak Titmice (*below*), White-breasted Nuthatches, Bewick's Wrens, Lazuli Buntings, Lark Sparrows, Chipping Sparrows, California Towhees, Spotted Towhees, Bullock's Orioles, Brown-headed Cowbirds, Western Meadowlarks, and Lesser Goldfinches. In and adja-cent to the riparian habitat in the immediate area watch for White-tailed

The flash of rufous in wing and tail announce the presence of the Ash-throated Flycatcher among the oaks.

Pairs of Oak Titmice quietly search the oaks for a meal.

Kites, Black Phoebes, Western Warbling Vireos, Wrentits, Cedar Waxwings, Yellow-breasted Chats, Yellow Warblers, and Black-headed Grosbeaks. Lewis's Woodpeckers winter in the area.

To the south, not far into California, four more species from the California Floristic Province appear including Nuttall's Woodpeckers, California Thrashers, Black-chinned Sparrows, and Lawrence's Goldfinches.

HIGH DESERT

The high desert lies in the rain shadow of the Cascades, and some people use adjectives like "desolate," "barren," and "boring" to describe the scenery. However, these are typically people who have not left the paved roads or stepped out of their vehicle. A pair of boots and a walk along the rimrock or up a ravine or into the isolated mountains reveal a diverse and magical world. This area supports a unique set of species among the wide expanse of sage flats, rimrock-lined streams and rivers, bunchgrass-covered hillsides, stands of aspens (*Populus tremuloides*) in the mountains, and juniper woodlands.

Some of the best places to seek these birds include the area around Fort Rock State Park and Hart Mountain National Antelope Refuge. The area is home to Chukar, Greater Sage-Grouse, Swainson's Hawks, Ferruginous Hawks, Red-tailed Hawks, Golden Eagles (*right*), American Kestrels, Prairie Falcons, Common Nighthawks, Common Poorwills, Gray Flycatchers, Western Kingbirds, Horned Larks, Loggerhead Shrikes, Common Ravens, Black-billed Magpies, Sage Thrashers, Mountain Bluebirds, Canyon Wrens (*right*), Lark Sparrows, Sagebrush Sparrows, Brewer's Sparrows, Vesper Sparrows, and Western Meadowlarks. In winter Rough-legged Hawks and Northern Shrikes visit.

Golden Eagles are most often seen soaring high over their territory or perched on utility poles.

Canyon Wrens announce their presence with a distinctive descending song.

Checklist of the Birds of Crater Lake National Park

Taxonomy from the Checklist of North American Birds, 7th edition, and its supplements published by the American Ornithological Society. Checklist updated from Farner (1952) and Follett (1978).

KEY

Primary Habitat

Lk   Lake
Ri   Riparian
Ro   Outcrops, rim
Me   Meadows
Fir   True fir/Douglas-fir forest
PP   Ponderosa pine forest
LP   Lodgepole pine forest
Sh   Shrubland
Ae   Aerial, most often seen flying over the park

Abundance

a   Abundant (can be observed on nearly every
    visit in the appropriate season)
c   Common (can be observed on more than
    half the visits in the appropriate season)
u   Uncommon (can be observed on less than
    half the visits in the appropriate season)
r   Rare (can be observed on less than 10% of
    visits to the park)

Note that at higher elevations populations tend to vary
annually more than in other locations.

Seasonal Occurrence

Spring   April–May
Summer   June–early August
Fall   late August–October
Winter   November–March

Species	Habitat	Spring	Summer	Fall	Winter
Ducks, geese, and swans (Anatidae)					
Greater White-fronted Goose	Ae	u		u	
Snow Goose	Ae	r		r	
Canada Goose	Ae, Lk	u	r	u	
Tundra Swan	Ae	r		r	
Wood Duck	Ri	r	r	r	
Gadwall	Lk	r		r	
American Wigeon	Lk	r		r	
Mallard	Ri	r	u	r	
Cinnamon Teal	Lk	r		r	
Northern Shoveler	Lk	r	r	r	
Northern Pintail	Lk	r	r	r	
Green-winged Teal	Lk	r		r	
Canvasback	Lk	r	r	r	
Redhead	Lk	r	r	r	
Ring-necked Duck	Lk	r		r	
Lesser Scaup	Lk	r	r	r	
Bufflehead	Lk	r		r	
Barrow's Goldeneye	Lk	r	r	r	r
Hooded Merganser	Lk		r	r	
Common Merganser	Lk	r	c	c	
Ruddy Duck	Lk	r	r	r	r
New World Quail (Odontophoridae)					
California Quail	Ri	r	r	r	
Mountain Quail	Fir	u	u	u	u
Grouse, pheasant, and allies (Phasianidae)					
Ruffed Grouse	Ri	u	u	u	u
Sooty Grouse	Fir, Me	c	c	c	c

Species	Habitat	Spring	Summer	Fall	Winter
Grebes (Podicipedidae)					
Pied-billed Grebe	Lk	r	r	r	
Horned Grebe	Lk			r	
Eared Grebe	Lk		r	r	
Western Grebe	Lk	r		r	
Pigeons and doves (Columbidae)					
Mourning Dove	PP	u	u	u	
Nighthawks, whip-poor-wills, and allies (Caprimulgidae)					
Common Nighthawk	PP, Ae		c	c	
Common Poorwill	PP		r	r	
Swifts (Apodidae)					
Black Swift	Ae			r	
Vaux's Swift	Ae	r	c	c	
Hummingbirds (Trochilidae)					
Anna's Hummingbird	Me		r	r	
Calliope Hummingbird	Me		r	r	
Rufous Hummingbird	Me		c	c	
Coots, rails, and allies (Rallidae)					
American Coot	Lk	r	r	r	
Cranes (Gruidae)					
Sandhill Crane	Ae	r		r	
Plovers and allies (Charadriidae)					
Black-bellied Plover	Lk	r		r	
Killdeer	Lk	r	r	r	
Semipalmated Plover	Lk	r		r	
Sandpipers and allies (Scolopacidae)					
Wilson's Snipe	Ri	r	r	r	
Spotted Sandpiper	Lk		c	c	

Species	Habitat	Spring	Summer	Fall	Winter
Solitary Sandpiper	Lk		r	r	
Greater Yellowlegs	Lk			r	
Wilson's Phalarope	Lk		r	r	
Gulls, terns, and allies (Laridae)					
Ring-billed Gull	Lk		r	r	
California Gull	Lk		c	c	
Loons (Gaviidae)					
Common Loon	Lk	r	r	r	
Cormorants (Phalacrocoracidae)					
Double-crested Cormorant	Lk		u	u	
Pelicans (Pelecanidae)					
American White Pelican	Lk	r	r	r	
Herons, egrets, and allies (Ardeidae)					
Great Blue Heron	Ri	r	r	r	
Great Egret	Ri		r		
Black-crowned Night Heron	Ri		r		
New World Vultures (Cathartidae)					
Turkey Vulture	Ae	u	u	u	
Osprey (Pandionidae)					
Osprey	Lk, Ae		r	r	
Hawks, eagles, and allies (Accipitridae)					
Golden Eagle	Ae	r	u	u	r
Northern Harrier	Ae		r	u	
Sharp-shinned Hawk	Fir	r	u	u	
Cooper's Hawk	Fir, PP	r	u	u	
American Goshawk	PP, Fir	r	r	r	r
Bald Eagle	Lk	r	u	u	r
Red-shouldered Hawk	Ae			r	

Species	Habitat	Spring	Summer	Fall	Winter
Swainson's Hawk	Ae		r	r	
Red-tailed Hawk	Me, Ae	u	c	c	r
Rough-legged Hawk	Ae	r		r	r
Ferruginous Hawk	Ae	r		r	
Typical Owls (Strigidae)					
Flammulated Owl	PP			r	
Western Screech-Owl	Ri	r	r	r	r
Great Horned Owl	PP, Fir	u	u	u	u
Northern Pygmy-Owl	Fir	u	u	r	r
Spotted Owl	Fir	r	r	r	r
Barred Owl	Fir	r	r	r	r
Great Gray Owl	PP, Fir	r	r	r	r
Long-eared Owl	Ri	r	r	r	
Northern Saw-whet Owl	Fir	r	r	r	r
Kingfishers (Alcedinidae)					
Belted Kingfisher	Lk, Ri	r	r	r	r
Woodpeckers (Picidae)					
Lewis's Woodpecker	Ae	r	r	u	
Williamson's Sapsucker	PP, Fir	r	u	u	
Red-breasted Sapsucker	Fir	c	c	c	
American Three-toed Woodpecker	LP	r	r	r	r
Black-backed Woodpecker	LP	u	u	u	u
Downy Woodpecker	Ri	r	r	r	
Hairy Woodpecker	Fir	c	c	c	c
White-headed Woodpecker	PP	u	u	u	u
Northern Flicker	PP, Fir	c	c	c	r
Pileated Woodpecker	Fir	u	u	u	u

Species	Habitat	Spring	Summer	Fall	Winter
Falcons and allies (Falconidae)					
American Kestrel	Me	u	u	u	
Merlin	Ae			r	
Peregrine Falcon	Ae, Ro	r	r	r	
Prairie Falcon	Ae		r	r	
Flycatchers (Tyrannidae)					
Ash-throated Flycatcher	PP		r		
Western Kingbird	Me		r		
Olive-sided Flycatcher	Fir	u	c		
Western Wood-Pewee	PP	u	u	u	
Willow Flycatcher	Ri	r	r	r	
Hammond's Flycatcher	Fir	u	c	u	
Dusky Flycatcher	Sh	u	c	u	
Western Flycatcher	Fir	u	c	u	
Say's Phoebe	Me	r		r	
Vireos (Vireonidae)					
Cassin's Vireo	PP, Fir	u	u	u	
Western Warbling Vireo	Ri	u	u	u	
Crows, jays and allies (Corvidae)					
Canada Jay	Fir	c	c	c	c
Steller's Jay	Fir, PP	a	a	a	c
California Scrub-Jay	Ri			r	
Clark's Nutcracker	Me, Ro	a	a	a	c
Black-billed Magpie	Ri	r	r	r	r
American Crow	Me		r		
Common Raven	Ae, Ro	a	a	a	c

Species	Habitat	Spring	Summer	Fall	Winter
Chickadees and titmice (Paridae)					
Black-capped Chickadee	Ri	r	r	r	r
Mountain Chickadee	Fir	a	a	a	a
Chestnut-backed Chickadee	Fir	u	u	u	u
Oak Titmouse	Ri		r		
Larks (Alaudidae)					
Horned Lark	Me	r	u	u	r
Swallows and martins (Hirundinidae)					
Violet-green Swallow	Lk, Ri	u	c	u	
Barn Swallow	Ri	r	r	r	
Bushtits (Aegithalidae)					
Bushtit	Ri	r	r	r	
Kinglets (Regulidae)					
Ruby-crowned Kinglet	LP, Fir	u	u	u	r
Golden-crowned Kinglet	Fir	a	a	a	c
Waxwings (Bombycillidae)					
Cedar Waxwing	Ri	r		r	
Nuthatches (Sittidae)					
Red-breasted Nuthatch	Fir	a	a	a	a
White-breasted Nuthatch	PP	u	u	u	u
Pygmy Nuthatch	PP	r	r	r	
Creepers (Certhiidae)					
Brown Creeper	Fir	c	c	c	c
Wrens (Troglodytidae)					
Rock Wren	Ro	u	c	c	
Bewick's Wren	Ri		r		
Northern House Wren	PP	r	r	r	
Pacific Wren	Fir	c	c	c	u

Species	Habitat	Spring	Summer	Fall	Winter
Dippers (Cinclidae)					
American Dipper	Ri, Lk	c	c	c	c
Thrushes, bluebirds, and allies (Turdidae)					
Western Bluebird	PP	r	r	r	
Mountain Bluebird	Me	u	c	c	
Townsend's Solitaire	Fir, PP	u	u	u	r
Swainson's Thrush	Ri		c	r	
Hermit Thrush	Fir	c	a	c	
American Robin	Fir, PP	c	c	c	r
Varied Thrush	Fir	c	u	c	
Pipits and wagtails (Motacillidae)					
American Pipit	Me	r		u	
Finches and allies (Fringillidae)					
Evening Grosbeak	Fir, PP	u	u	u	r
Gray-crowned Rosy-Finch	Ri, Me	u	c	u	r
House Finch	Ri	r		r	
Purple Finch	Fir	r	r	r	
Cassin's Finch	Fir, PP	a	a	a	r
Redpoll	Ri				r
Red Crossbill	Fir, PP	c	c	c	u
Pine Siskin	Fir, LP	a	a	c	r
Lesser Goldfinch	Me			r	
American Goldfinch	Me		r	r	
Sparrows, towhees, and allies (Passerellidae)					
Lark Sparrow	Me	r		r	
Chipping Sparrow	Me	c	c	c	
Fox Sparrow	Sh	u	u	u	
Dark-eyed Junco	Fir, LP, PP	a	a	a	u

Species	Habitat	Spring	Summer	Fall	Winter
White-crowned Sparrow	Me, Ri	u	u	c	
Golden-crowned Sparrow	Ri	u		u	
Vesper Sparrow	Me		r	r	
Savannah Sparrow	Me	r		r	
Song Sparrow	Ri	r	r	r	
Lincoln's Sparrow	Ri	r	c	c	
Green-tailed Towhee	Sh	u	u	u	
Spotted Towhee	Sh, Ri	r			
Blackbirds, orioles, and allies (Icteridae)					
Red-winged Blackbird	Ri	r	r	r	
Brown-headed Cowbird	Ri		r	r	
Brewer's Blackbird	Ri, Me	r	r	r	
Western Meadowlark	Me	r		r	
Wood-warblers (Parulidae)					
Orange-crowned Warbler	Ri	r	u	u	
Nashville Warbler	Sh	u	c	c	
MacGillivray's Warbler	Ri	u	c	c	
Yellow-rumped Warbler	Fir, LP, PP	a	a	a	r
Yellow Warbler	Ri	r	r		
Black-throated Gray Warbler	Sh, PP	r		r	
Townsend's Warbler	Fir	u	r	u	
Hermit Warbler	Fir	c	c	u	
Wilson's Warbler	Ri	u	u	u	
Cardinals, bunting, tanagers, and allies (Cardinalidae)					
Western Tanager	Fir, PP	a	a	a	
Black-headed Grosbeak	Ri, Fir	r	u	u	
Lazuli Bunting	Ri	r	c	c	

Additional species that have been observed one or a few times in Crater Lake National Park. Not likely to be observed.

Brant
Blue-winged Teal
Common Goldeneye
Ring-necked Pheasant
Red-necked Grebe
Rock Pigeon
Band-tailed Pigeon
White-throated Swift
Black-chinned Hummingbird
Ruddy Turnstone
Wandering Tattler
Black Tern
Forster's Tern
Western Gull
Brown Pelican
Red-naped Sapsucker
Red-eyed Vireo
Tree Swallow
Northern Rough-winged Swallow
Cliff Swallow
Bohemian Waxwing
European Starling
House Sparrow
Pine Grosbeak
White-winged Crossbill
American Tree Sparrow
Yellow-breasted Chat
Bullock's Oriole
Tricolored Blackbird
Tennessee Warbler

References and Suggested Readings

General References

Gabrielson, I. N., and S. G. Jewett. 1970. *Birds of the Pacific Northwest.* New York: Dover Publications. (Originally published as *Birds of Oregon*, 1940.)

Gill, F. B., R. O. Prum, and S. K. Robinson. 2019. *Ornithology.* 4th ed. New York: W. H. Freeman and Company.

Marshall, D. B., M. G. Hunter, and A. L. Contreras, eds. 2003. *Birds of Oregon: A General Reference.* Corvallis: Oregon State University Press.

Wells, J. V. 2007. *Birder's Conservation Handbook: 100 North American Birds at Risk.* New York: Princeton University Press.

Field Guides

Among the abundance of field guides to choose from, three of the most popular are suggested below.

Dunn, J. L., and J. Alderfer. 2017. *National Geographic Field Guide to Birds of North America.* 7th ed. Washington, DC: National Geographic Society.

Sibley, D. A. 2014. *The Sibley Guide to Birds.* 2nd ed. New York: National Audubon Society.

Sibley, D. A. 2016. *The Sibley Guide to Birds of Western North America.* 2nd ed. New York: Alfred A. Knopf.

Technical References

Buktenica, M. W. Ecology of kokanee salmon and rainbow trout in Crater Lake, a deep ultraoligotrophic caldera lake, Oregon. 1988. Master's thesis. Oregon State University, Corvallis.

Creeden, E. P., J. A. Hicke, and P. C. Buotte. 2014. Climate weather and recent mountain pine beetle outbreaks in the western United States. *Forest Ecology and Management* 312:1239–1251.

Farner, D. S. 1952. *The Birds of Crater Lake National Park.* Lawrence: University of Kansas Press.

Follett, D. 1979. *Birds of Crater Lake National Park.* Crater Lake Natural History Association. National Park Service. US Department of Interior.

Lanner, D. M. 1996. *Made for Each Other: A Symbiosis of Birds and Pines.* New York: Oxford University Press.

McKechnie, A. E., and B. G. Lovegrove. 2002. Avian facultative hypothermic responses: A review. *Condor* 104:705–724.

Merrill, J. C. 1888. Notes on the birds of Fort Klamath, Oregon. *Auk* 5:136–146, 251–262, 357–366.

Mohren, S., and J. Beck. 2015. Crater Lake National Park Terrestrial Ecology Branch 2014 Project summary. Department of Interior, National Park Service. 15 p.

Preisler, H. K., J. A. Hicke, A. A. Ager, and J. L. Hayes. 2012. Climate and weather influences on spatial temporal patterns of mountain pine beetle populations in Washington and Oregon. *Ecology* 93:2421–5434.

Schoettle, A. W. 2004. Developing Proactive Management Options to Sustain Bristlecone and Limber Pine Ecosystems in the Presence of a Non-Native Pathogen. In *Silviculture in Special Places: Proceedings of the National Silviculture Workshop*, compiled by W. D. Shepperd and L. G. Eskew, pp. 146–155. September 8–11, 2003. Proceedings RMRS-P-34. Fort Collins, CO: USDA Forest Service, Rocky Mountain Research Station.

Agencies and Organizations

A number of organizations and agencies work with birds regarding conservation, management, or public education in the general area of Crater Lake National Park. The following list provides contact information for some of these groups.

Crater Lake National Park
P. O. Box 7
Crater Lake, OR 97604-0007
541-594-3000
www.nps.gov/crla

Crater Lake Natural History Association
570 Rim Village Drive
Crater Lake, OR 97604
541-594-2356
www.craterlakeoregon.org

Friends of Crater Lake National Park
P. O. Box 88
Crater Lake, OR 97604
www.friendsofcraterlake.org

Rogue Valley Audubon Society
P. O. Box 8597
Medford, OR 97504
www.roguevalleyaudubon.org

Klamath Basin Audubon Society
P. O. Box 354
Klamath Falls, OR 97601
www.eaglecon.org

Umpqua Valley Audubon Society
P. O. Box 381
Roseburg, OR 97470
www.umpquavalleyaudubon.org

Siskiyou Audubon Society
www.siskiyouaudubon.org

Klamath Bird Observatory
541-201-0866
www.klamathbird.org

The Nature Conservancy
33 Central Avenue
Medford, OR 97501
541-770-7933
www.nature.org

Rogue/Siskiyou National Forest
333 W Eighth
Medford, OR 97501
541-858-2200
www.fs.fed.us/r6/rogue-siskiyou/contact

Umpqua National Forest
2900 Northwest Stewart Parkway
Roseburg, OR 97471
541-957-3495
www.fs.fed.us/r6/umpqua/contact

Fremont-Winema National Forest
1301 South G Street
Lakeview, OR 97630
541-947-2151
www.fs.fed.us/r6/frewin/contact

Klamath Basin National Wildlife Refuges
4009 Hill Road
Tulelake, CA 96134
530-667-2231
www.fws.gov/klamathbasinrefuges

Southern Oregon University
1250 Siskiyou Boulevard
Ashland, OR 97520
541-552-7672
www.sou.edu

Oregon Institute of Technology
3201 Campus Drive
Klamath Falls, OR 97601
541-885-1150
www.oit.edu

Index

Bolded entries indicate species accounts